C0-BWH-529

*JOHN MARSHALL*

*Westminster Press Books*
*by*
TERI MARTINI

*John Marshall*
*The Mystery of the Woman in the Mirror*
*Patrick Henry, Patriot*
*The Lucky Ghost Shirt*

# *John Marshall*

BY

TERI MARTINI

*Illustrated by Alex Stein*

THE WESTMINSTER PRESS

PHILADELPHIA

*Book Design by Dorothy Alden Smith*

Published by The Westminster Press ®
Philadelphia, Pennsylvania

PRINTED IN THE UNITED STATES OF AMERICA

**Library of Congress Cataloging in Publication Data**

Martini, Teri.
John Marshall.

Bibliography: p.
SUMMARY: A biography of the Chief Justice of the Supreme Court, first appointed by James Madison, who strengthened the court and made it a power that could balance the executive and legislative branches.
1. Marshall, John, 1755–1835—Juvenile literature. [1. Marshall, John, 1755–1835. 2. United States. Supreme Court—Biography] I. Stein, Alex, illus. II. Title.
E302.6.M4M36 347'.73'2634 [B] [92] 73-11430
ISBN 0-664-32540-8

*To Michael*
*with Love*

# *Contents*

Chapter 1

# *The Trick*

John Marshall left the house quickly. He stopped only long enough to pick up his rifle. He always carried the gun when he traveled through the forests. Bears and wolves were often seen in the hills of Virginia. It was best to be prepared.

Sixteen years before, when John was born on September 24, 1755, these woods had been considered the wilderness. Now farmers like John's father were moving in and pushing west.

Whistling softly to himself, John set out to hike the miles that separated the Marshalls' home on Goose Creek from their neighbors. He was sure that his younger brothers and sisters would be busy for hours. Not one of them even had asked to tag along. That was because they were searching for a strawberry patch.

John had written clues to the location of the strawberries in rhyme. The youngsters were so anxious to solve the puzzle, they did not even notice when their oldest brother left.

After more than an hour of hiking, John found his friend waiting.

"Hello, Peter," called John cheerfully.

Peter waved, but he looked far from cheerful. John was surprised. The boys lived so far apart that it was difficult to meet very often, and Peter was usually happy to see him.

"I'm glad you've come," said Peter, hurrying toward John.

"You don't look it. What's wrong?"

Both boys were sixteen, but John was much taller. He was dark-haired and lean, while Peter was shorter, but heavier. Peter had fair hair and a round, honest face. Farm work had helped develop his muscles. John had a difficult time holding his own against Peter in wrestling matches.

"Everything's wrong," said Peter. "We have a visitor. My cousin from Williamsburg got here yesterday."

John had never been to the city. "Why, he could be very interesting, Peter!"

"Not this fellow!"

John gave his friend a searching look. "What's the matter with him?"

"We're not sure," said Peter.

"You're not sure! Well, what kind of boy is he?" demanded John.

Peter shrugged helplessly. "Solemn," he said finally. "He hasn't smiled since he got here."

"H'mm," said John. That did not sound promising.

"That's why I'm glad you've come," said Peter. "We're depending on you."

"To do what?"

"To talk to him," said Peter. "He's educated. Went to William and Mary College for a while. You know none of us can read like you. We don't know what to say to him."

It was true that the members of the Marshall family were unusual. Unlike their neighbors, all of them could read and write. None of the children had ever been to school, but Thomas and Mary Marshall taught each one at home.

"Knowing how to read doesn't mean you can perform miracles," John warned.

Peter paid no attention. He was sure that John could charm anyone.

"I knew you would be willing to help," he said.

"Let's have a look at the fellow," said John.

As the boys came near Peter's house, John saw the cousin sitting under a tree. He wore a plain black suit and certainly looked different from the sun-tanned, country boys. Their breeches were buckskin, and each wore a colorful, fringed hunting shirt.

When Peter introduced the boys, Charles Johnson stood politely.

"Your servant, Mr. Marshall," said the young man gravely and bowed.

Not to be outdone, John bowed too, but awkwardly.

"A pleasure, Mr. Johnson," he said.

Charles looked to be about seventeen, but he acted much older. John smiled.

"I understand you are from Williamsburg, Mr. Johnson. It must be exciting to live in a city," he said, hoping to draw the young man out.

But Charles only nodded and said softly, "Yes."

There was a long pause while the boys stared uncomfortably at one another. John searched about in his mind for something to say, but he could think of nothing. He was seldom at a loss for words. Charles was certainly having a strange effect. And the fellow was solemn, just as Peter had said.

John decided on a different approach. "Well, Mr. Johnson, can we interest you in a game of quoits?" he suggested, smiling once more.

When John saw Peter's horrified expression, the smile nearly froze on his lips.

"Oh, John, Charles would not be interested in quoits! You forget, he is from the city. And he has studied to be a *minister.*" Peter carefully emphasized the last word. "He's practically a man of God," he added.

John didn't see how that would prevent Charles from enjoying a game of quoits. Still, he was willing to give up the idea, if Peter thought it would offend his cousin.

But Charles surprised them both. "As a matter of fact, I'd like to play."

"You would?" Peter was astonished.

"Yes, we have some acquaintance with the game in the city," replied Charles.

John grinned, triumphant, and led the way to the quoit court Peter and he had made. Politely John offered his opponent the choice of quoits. When Charles made his selection of the round, iron rings, he did not first test their weight and balance. John was sure he would have little trouble winning the match.

Peter hovered beside them. "Charles, are you familiar with the rules?" he asked.

John wished Peter would stop worrying so much about offending his cousin. Maybe a game was just what Charles needed to cheer him up.

"Perhaps you would like to review them for me," replied Charles.

"Well, this is the pitcher's box," explained Peter. "It's forty feet from the stake. The object of the game is to circle the stake with your quoit. If neither of you does this, the quoit nearest the stake wins the point."

"I see," said Charles. "Will you toss first or shall I, Mr. Marshall?"

"Oh, the honor is yours," said John, trying to match Charles's excellent manners.

Charles removed his jacket and took his place in the pitcher's box. He tossed a quoit, which sailed gracefully through the air and firmly circled the stake.

"Oh, that is very good." Peter made a point of complimenting his cousin.

Charles rolled his eyes toward heaven. " 'All gifts cometh from the Lord,' " he said.

John gave the young man a startled glance. The last time he had heard that particular phrase was in church. It didn't seem suitable here on the quoit court.

After the first round, John was one point behind, but he was not worried. Beginner's luck seldom lasted.

Moving to the opposite post, the boys tossed their quoits again. This time John was more careful and had two ringers.

"Don't be discouraged, Charles," said Peter quickly. "None of us can beat John. He's a champion."

Charles shrugged. " 'Fight the good fight,' " he said.

Another pious remark? Behind Charles's back, John and Peter exchanged a look of complete disgust. Didn't Charles ever relax and enjoy himself?

The game continued, and the score remained very close indeed. John became too busy trying to win to puzzle over Charles's annoying behavior.

When the boys tossed their quoits for the deciding point, both looked equally close to the stake. To John's surprise, Charles suddenly claimed victory. He held out his hand.

"I'm sorry you lost, Mr. Marshall. You played very well. My congratulations."

This was too much for John. He had had enough of politeness. He was angry! You would think a fellow like Charles, who was given to quoting the Bible, might be a little more humble.

"Hold on a moment," cried John. "I'm not altogether certain my quoit is not closer than yours. I'll measure."

Peter agreed at once, but still tried to soothe his cousin's feelings. "I hope you won't mind, but we always do measure to be sure."

"Ah!" mourned Charles. " 'Blessed are they that have not seen, and yet have believed.' Gather the evidence then."

John thought that if Charles left the farm tomorrow, it would not be too soon. Frowning, he plucked two blades of grass. On hands and knees, he bent over the quoits, measuring with care. At last he rose and walked slowly back to Charles.

"What is the verdict?" asked the young man.

"You won!" announced John, awe mingled with disbelief in his tone.

"He won!" echoed Peter. "Charles, you're a beginner, and you beat John!"

Something seemed to be wrong. Charles was having trouble controlling himself. Was he angry? No! He threw back his head and laughed heartily for the first time that afternoon. The other boys stared as though Charles had suddenly gone mad.

"Beginner! Who's a beginner?" asked Charles at last.

Reaching inside his pocket, he withdrew a heavy medal.

"Winner at Quoits—County Championship 1771," read John.

"You tricked us!" he cried. His dark eyes flashed with anger.

Charles was not disturbed. "Ah, John, trickery was the farthest thing from my mind. It was modesty. Yes, it was modesty that would not permit me to mention my dubious honor," he protested.

"Modesty!" sputtered John.

"Modesty!" repeated Charles gravely, and then he spoiled the effect with a grin.

"Well, I'll be!" cried John.

Charles threw an arm around each boy. Together they laughed until they were weak. It was a good joke, and the younger boys had been taken in.

"Oh, Charles," gasped Peter, "I owe you an apology. You don't know the terrible things I've been thinking about you."

"I know exactly what you have been thinking, Peter. That I was a bookish bore who was going to spoil your fun. And you couldn't wait to get rid of me. I just thought I would give you a taste of what you thought I was like."

"How about a rematch?" asked John.

"Why not?" replied Charles. "I'll even give you a two-point handicap."

"Make it five," said John.

Charles looked shocked. "Would you take advantage of a man of God?"

"No, but a tricky county champion is another matter," said John, laughing.

The boys rolled up their sleeves and began to play in earnest.

CHAPTER 2

# *The Battle of Great Bridge*

WHEN JOHN WAS eighteen, the growing Marshall family moved from their small cabin in The Hollow. Thomas Marshall built a handsome frame house at Oak Hill, not far away. It was the largest house for miles around. There were two stories and seven big rooms. What comfort the Marshalls could enjoy! They were the envy of all their neighbors.

But what noise and confusion the Marshalls could create! John Marshall often complained these days. There were eleven children now and no really quiet place for a serious young man of nineteen to study.

"Oh, forget your musty, old law books," young Thomas would say, flexing his muscles. "Come out and wrestle."

"Haven't time," John usually replied.

To his brother's great disgust, John would retire to the house, but not to study law.

John let his family think studying law was his purpose. Carefully, he would open an impressive volume of Blackstone's *Commentaries on Law* and prop it up in front of him. Inside the large journal, he opened a smaller book. It was in this book that he quickly became absorbed.

When Elizabeth came to John's door one afternoon with the news that Father had returned from Richmond, she was completely fooled. If John had not dropped the books in his excitement, she would never have known.

John bent to pick them up, but Elizabeth was quicker. She stood with the *Manual of Arms* in her small hands.

"So, you do think there will be war, John," she accused him. "This is a book of military exercises."

While Father was away, John had tried to keep his worst fears from the women of the family. He especially did not want Elizabeth to know. The idea of war terrified her.

"Yes, I'm afraid so," said John. "I've already had word that they will be organizing a unit of Culpeper Minutemen."

"And you'll go, I suppose?" demanded Elizabeth, her voice rising.

"Yes," said John. "King George has gone too far. He will not listen to reason. We must fight for our rights as free Englishmen."

"Rights!" Elizabeth's voice was shrill. Tears of fear and rage spilled down her flushed cheeks. "That's what I think of your rights!" she cried. Throwing the book across the room, she rushed away sobbing.

John shook his head and looked helplessly after her. There was nothing he could do for Elizabeth. She would have to find courage in her own way.

He hurried downstairs to greet his father. Thomas Marshall was sitting on the porch among some anxious farmers. He represented these men in the House of Burgesses. He had been away in Richmond at an important convention. There, among such leaders as George Washington and James Madison, he had listened to Patrick Henry plead with Virginians to get ready for war with England.

" 'Liberty or death!' That's what he said," Thomas Marshall told his friends. " 'Give me liberty or give me death!' I voted to arm. Mr. Henry is right. We have got to get about the business of defending ourselves."

While Thomas Marshall went inside to wash away the dust of his journey, John talked with the men about plans to defend Virginia from the King's soldiers.

"What will happen when Governor Dunmore learns of our decision?" asked one of the farmers. "He has spies everywhere. Our arms are stored at Williamsburg. The Governor already controls the city. He could easily steal our supplies. What can we do?"

No one knew what to say.

Several weeks later Governor Dunmore did steal Virginia's guns and ammunition. Patrick Henry knew what to do. The Culpeper Minutemen received a message to march against the English governor.

"Please don't go, John," begged Elizabeth.

She stood in the doorway of her brother's room as he gathered his things together.

"I must," he told her.

Elizabeth whirled about. "Go! Go and be killed! I don't care," she cried hysterically.

They were harsh, bitter words. John knew his sister did not mean them, but she was unable to control her fear.

No one else in the family behaved like Elizabeth. Mary Keith Marshall hated to see her son go. Still, she knew he was a man now and like other Virginians, he must do what he felt was right.

Everyone was up early the day John left. All except the very smallest children were outside to see him off. Elizabeth was not there. John did not like to leave without seeing her, but there was nothing he could do.

When he reached a little rise in the road, John turned for one last look at Oak Hill. At that moment Elizabeth rushed from the house. In most unladylike fashion, she held up her skirts and ran after John. When she reached him, Elizabeth thrust a small bundle into her brother's hands.

"John, forgive me. I didn't mean what I said," she told him in a choked voice. "Godspeed," she added.

Without waiting for a reply, she turned back. John watched her slow progress toward the house. Then he rode on.

He had not gone far when curiosity overcame him. He stopped and opened the bundle. Inside was his blue hunting shirt. Across the front Elizabeth had embroidered the words, "Liberty or Death."

John smiled.

"Oh, Elizabeth! You did find courage," he whispered.

John was appointed Lieutenant of the Culpeper Minutemen. Some of the men, like Peter, were old

friends. Others, John had never seen before. They came from three counties.

Lieutenant Marshall led his men to Williamsburg. The Culpeper Minutemen were an odd-looking group of soldiers. They carried guns, hunting knives, and tomahawks. Their hair was long and untidy. John's was not the only shirt embroidered with the words, "Liberty or Death." Many people were frightened by the sight of the Culpeper unit because they looked so unruly.

The men were ready for a fight, but outside Williamsburg, they met disappointment. An officer in the militia arrived with unexpected news.

"Mr. Henry has persuaded the Governor to pay for the arms he stole."

"Pay? You mean money?" shouted one of the angry Culpeper men.

"Yes, and he paid all that was asked," said the officer.

"I'd like to make him pay with more than money," grumbled Peter.

There were others who felt the same way. They stayed with John and camped outside the city. The "shirt men," as Governor Dunmore called them, had no immediate plans. But they worried the Governor so much that he finally fled from the city in the middle of the night.

"Let's go after him. We've got him on the run," cried the "shirt men."

John soon found this was not the case at all.

"Governor Dunmore and his men are quite safe beyond the Great Bridge at Norfolk. He has pronounced all men traitors who do not support him and His Majesty's cause," John reported. "There is only one approach to the fort. That is over a swamp. The British could shoot us for target practice in that open area if we tried to attack."

"Isn't anyone going to try?" demanded Peter.

"A regiment is moving in now. Shall we join them?" asked John.

The Culpeper Minutemen marched on to Norfolk. There the Virginia militia under Colonel William Woodford was camping in the mud.

Lieutenant Marshall led his men to the Colonel's tent to report for duty. Before John reached the Colonel, he saw a familiar figure.

"Father," called John. "I never expected to see you here."

Thomas Marshall threw his arm affectionately across his son's shoulders.

"Never expected to be here myself," replied the Major. "Colonel Woodford had need of all the men he could get. He called up our unit. But it is an impossible situation. We have no cannon. The Governor's fort is beyond the range of our guns. I don't think the British are going to oblige us by marching out to meet our men. But perhaps we can come up with a plan."

John and his men looked across at the makeshift British fort.

"The English have several hundred men there," said Major Marshall. "And that includes all the loyalists for miles around, as well as the slaves they have freed."

Peter looked at John's father. "But we must have over five hundred men ourselves, sir," he said. "We could surely overwhelm the British, if only they would come out."

"Yes, *if*, Peter. It is not likely that Dunmore will send anyone out as long as he knows he is outnumbered," said John.

"As long as he knows he is outnumbered," repeated Major Marshall slowly.

That night John's father went to Colonel Woodford with a plan.

"My Negro servant Ben has been with me a long time," he told the Colonel. "He is loyal, and he has great courage. If you are willing, Ben has agreed to take part in an attempt to trick the British into leaving their fort."

"What do you have in mind?" asked Colonel Woodford.

"Ben can make his way into the enemy camp. He will say he is a runaway slave come to join Governor Dunmore. Then he'll give the Governor false information. He'll swear that there are not more than three hundred soldiers in this camp."

Colonel Woodford stared into the fire. The chill of the December night was keenly felt in the damp air.

"It might work," said the Colonel. "It's worth a try." He looked up at Thomas Marshall. "Does your man understand the danger? There's little hope we could save him, if he were caught. It would probably mean his life."

The Major's jaw formed a firm, tight line. "Ben understands. He hopes to escape during the confusion of battle."

"He's a brave man," said Colonel Woodford. "Send him with my blessing."

That night a dark figure crept out of camp. Silently he made his way, circling far to the north and then back as one might if he were escaping. Only a few of the officers knew of the plan. Not even John was aware of the brave effort Ben was making for the Virginia patriots.

The Culpeper Minutemen slept soundly that night, but they were awakened at dawn by the noise of gunfire. The plan had worked! The British grenadiers were descending upon the camp.

Sleepy soldiers scrambled out of tents and manned the guns. As the British in their bright-red uniforms marched along the open causeway, six abreast, the men of the Virginia militia fired with deadly accuracy. These men of the frontier were experienced hunters. Again and again, their bullets found the target.

"They haven't a chance! What possessed the Governor to make such a blunder?" cried John.

Peter didn't know. He was too busy shooting and reloading his musket to answer.

It was the first either of the young men had seen of war. The battle was bloody. Nearly a hundred grenadiers were killed, including their captain. Not one of the Virginians was lost.

The colonial troops marched over the Great Bridge and into Norfolk while Governor Dunmore fled to the safety of his ships in the harbor.

John didn't feel like joining in the celebration afterward. Peter found him warming his hands by a fire.

"Are you ill, John?" asked Peter. "You weren't wounded."

"No, no," John assured him. "It isn't that. I've been thinking about Elizabeth. She seemed to have a better understanding of what war is than I did."

John looked down at the shirt his sister had so carefully embroidered. "Liberty or Death," he sighed. "War is not high spirits and passionate speeches. It's killing and dying!"

"With just cause," cried Peter. "You said so yourself, John. Freedom is worth the price. Have you changed your mind?"

John got to his feet. "Certainly not! What started me on this gloomy talk? Isn't anyone interested in racing or jumping? I'll challenge any man. I can jump twice my height."

"Twice your height!" Peter was surprised.

John laughed, then gazed at his friend slyly. "What's wrong? Don't you think I can do it?"

Peter looked shocked. "I would never wager against you, John," he said quickly.

John grinned. "Well, then, let's find someone who will," he said, his good humor restored.

The young men went off to join their comrades.

In the confusion of battle, Ben had managed to escape.

Over and over again, he had to tell the story of the way Lord Dunmore's men had been tricked.

The Battle of Great Bridge gave the Virginians confidence. Seven months later it was a Virginian, Richard Henry Lee, who proposed independence from England. It was a Virginian, Thomas Jefferson, who wrote the Declaration of Independence. It was Thomas Marshall's good friend, George Washington, another Virginian, who was named Commander in Chief of the Continental armies.

Both Thomas Marshall and his son John volunteered to serve under General Washington. The Culpeper Minutemen put aside their hunting shirts. Instead, they wore buff-and-blue uniforms and tricornered hats. But their motto was still, "Liberty or Death!"

Chapter 3

# *Soldier of the Revolution*

Lieutenant John Marshall was a good officer. Even when the Army was in retreat, he kept his courage and cheerful humor. He inspired his men. Within two years after the Battle of Great Bridge, John had been promoted to Captain-lieutenant and stationed with General Washington at Valley Forge.

The winter of 1777 was bitter and the men suffered greatly from lack of warm clothing and good food. One December afternoon John sat in his hut with nothing more than a tattered wool blanket to keep him warm.

He dipped his quill pen into an inkstand he had set on his log table. As Deputy Judge Advocate of the Army, John was preparing a written decision on a dispute he had been called upon to judge.

Lieutenant Philip Slaughter poked his head through the doorway of the wooden hut. John looked up from his writing. "Is it dry yet?" he asked.

"In a way," answered Lieutenant Slaughter evasively.

"In a way!" John exclaimed. "How long does it

take? A man could freeze to death while waiting for his shirt to dry. Did you hang it near the fire?"

Earlier that morning John had washed his only shirt. Like most of the soldiers at Valley Forge, Pennsylvania, John had little more than the clothes on his back. Many of the men were in rags. Some had no shoes and tied their feet up in cloth for some protection from the frozen ground.

In letter after letter General Washington begged the Continental Congress for money and supplies for his army. Congress in turn urged the states to outfit their own regiments. Most of the states ignored these requests. The soldiers continued to go in rags.

"I said, Did you hang it near the fire?" John asked again.

But Lieutenant Slaughter had gone. In his place John's shirt appeared, propped on a stick. The sleeves were spread out as they had hung on the line. The shirt was frozen solid.

John nearly groaned aloud. But then his dark eyes twinkled mischievously. He knew Lieutenant Slaughter was just outside the door awaiting a reaction. Probably Lieutenants Porterfield and Johnson were with him.

John addressed the shirt in a brisk tone.

"Well, well, soldier, what is your complaint?" asked John.

When there was no reply, John persisted. "Come, come, speak up, man. What is the trouble? You do look very thin. What have you been eating?"

"Fire cake and water!" cried John, as though horrified by the imaginary answer. "Look here, my man, this will never do. You've got to get hold of some meat. Meat and potatoes, that's what you need. Fried chicken and dumplings is the meal for you. No more of this fire cake and water," he added.

John was about to go on, but the groans of his messmates and the sudden withdrawal of his frozen shirt stopped him. He went to the door and looked outside. His fellow officers were moaning and clutching their empty stomachs.

"How could you, Captain?" groaned Philip. "I'd all but forgotten there was any other kind of food but fire cake and water."

The young lieutenant was talking about the soggy

dough that the soldiers warmed over their fires for dinner. It had been a long time since any of them had had any other food. Supplies were very low.

"Fried chicken and dumplings!" cried Lieutenant Johnson.

"Potatoes," groaned Lieutenant Porterfield.

They gazed accusingly at John.

John ignored them and went directly to his frozen shirt, which was now leaning dejectedly against the hut.

While the Army was camped for the winter, there was little for the soldiers to do but play pranks on one another.

The war was not going well for the Americans. In September of 1777, they had been defeated at Brandywine Creek. Fortunately, the Americans won a victory at Saratoga, New York, later in the fall. But winter was a bleak and depressing time.

In the spring of 1778, spirits began to rise again. Cheerful and energetic as ever, John began organizing games and contests among his fellow officers. He had received a package from home in which he found a new pair of blue socks with white heels.

"Now that is something to boast about," John confided to Philip.

"Socks with white heels, Captain?" Philip looked doubtful. "Shouldn't they be all one color?"

"Certainly not," said John. "These are distinctive," he added proudly.

It wasn't long before the men became very familiar with those heels. John could outjump and outrun all the other young officers. The one thing the men saw again and again was John's heels. Silverheels, they nicknamed him. When Washington's Army left Valley Forge that spring, the men were determined to defeat the British.

John was in the hard-fought Battle of Monmouth in June. Although neither side claimed victory, the Americans were encouraged. They had held their own.

John spent another winter with the Army. Then the troops moved to New York. Here, John was with a special unit of light infantry that stormed and took Stony Point on the Hudson River.

In August of 1779, Captain Marshall was recalled to Virginia. He had to await the formation of a new regiment.

At Oak Hill, John found his mother and the younger children. His brother Thomas was away with a Virginia regiment. Colonel Marshall was stationed at Yorktown.

Elizabeth wept when she saw her older brother. "Thank heaven you are safe!" she cried, rushing into John's arms. "When will this terrible fighting end?"

"Soon, Elizabeth," John told her. "Very soon. The French, the Spanish, and now the Dutch have joined the war against the British. It is only a matter of time before we win our freedom."

"Not before I can get into the fight, I hope," said young James Marshall. Now sixteen and a member of the local militia, he was anxious to see action.

"No, probably not before then," said his brother.

He sighed. James would have to find out about war for himself.

In the evenings the Marshall home was filled with visitors. John told stories of his adventures and of the way the battles were going.

"Washington's Army is taking fort after fort along the Hudson. By summer we will have West Point too. It's the stronghold of the Hudson. From there we can control the whole river valley and cut off British supplies."

Early in 1780, John went to visit his father at Yorktown, Virginia. Colonel Marshall was not as enthusiastic about General Washington's victories along the Hudson.

"The South is the key now, John," he said. "General Cornwallis is in Georgia. The British have Savannah, and General Clinton is likely to sail from New York as soon as warm weather permits. If he ever captures the city of Charleston, we can expect he'll move north. There will be fighting on Virginia soil."

"Surely the French fleet will stop the British ships," protested John.

"That remains to be seen," said Colonel Marshall. "I think perhaps we rely too heavily upon French support. The French have not been able to recapture Savannah."

Then he changed the subject. "Enough of this war talk! It's mighty good to see you, John. You look fine too. A little thin, perhaps. But that's nothing the ladies of Yorktown can't cure with their fine meals."

John soon found himself invited to many balls and parties. Awkward and shy at first, he thought he would never learn to enjoy all the social activities.

Then he met Mary Ambler. Polly, as everyone called her, was dark-haired, extremely pretty, and as charmingly shy as John himself.

It wasn't long before the young captain became a constant visitor at the Ambler home. Soon John talked less and less about war and more about a peacetime career.

Colonel Marshall understood, and he did not disapprove. Polly would make a fine wife for John some day.

"You know, John, Williamsburg is only a few miles away. While you are waiting to be called back into service, you could go to college and continue your study of law. When the war is over, our country will have need of sound, legal thinking."

John enrolled at the College of William and Mary in May of 1780. Here he joined Chancellor George Wythe's law classes. John took careful notes in a leatherbound notebook, but thoughts of Polly kept interfering with his work. In the margins and on the cover he wrote her name. Miss Polly Ambler. Miss Maria. Polly!

A few weeks later, when the Amblers stopped at Williamsburg, John and his friends arranged a ball for Polly and her older sister, Eliza.

After the ball Polly and John strolled through the quiet streets.

"Papa has been made treasurer of the state," Polly announced unexpectedly. "He says we will move to Richmond."

She raised large, brown eyes to meet John's gaze. "How far away is Richmond, John?"

The thought of being separated from Polly terrified John. He came to an instant decision. "Too far!" he cried.

A few days later John Marshall left college and followed the Amblers.

John had little formal education. There were the six weeks at William and Mary and a few months at

boarding school when he was younger. Of course, he had done a great deal of reading on his own.

In Richmond, John went to his cousin, Thomas Jefferson, for a law license. Mr. Jefferson was then Governor of Virginia. He tested John and found him ready. That August of 1780, John was admitted to the bar in Fauquier County. Now, John thought, he could set up a law practice and marry Polly.

Before he could even get started, news of the British capture of Charleston, South Carolina, shocked everyone.

"We can expect an attack on Virginia next," Colonel Marshall told his son.

"Perhaps Governor Jefferson will raise troops, and I will be recalled to service," said John.

When he thought of all those he loved who would suffer if an invasion came, John was prepared to fight again. Anxiously he awaited a call to arms. But Governor Jefferson did not seem to be organizing any troops at all.

CHAPTER 4

# *Too Young for Politics*

BY LATE NOVEMBER of 1780, Governor Jefferson's failure to act was the talk of the Richmond tavern. The men sat at small tables in the comfortable common room. There, at the close of each day's session of the legislature, the members continued their debating. When John's father visited Richmond, he and John joined their friends at the tavern.

"What is the Governor waiting for?" a wealthy businessman wanted to know. "He could have five thousand men in a fortnight."

"Perhaps there is not so much danger as we think," said the speaker of the Virginia Assembly. William Henry Harrison was a calm, peaceful man.

"Nonsense!"

The voice of the great orator, Patrick Henry, filled the room. Everyone stopped to listen. Mr. Henry had been the first governor of Virginia. He spoke with authority. "What greater victory can there be for the English than to capture and hang the author of the Declaration of Independence? Make no mistake. There is serious danger."

The discussion was interrupted when a man entered the tavern. He must have been riding hard, for he could not seem to catch his breath. He held up a Philadelphia newspaper for all to see.

"Gentleman, I regret to announce—" He paused and went on in a choked voice. "General Benedict Arnold has turned against us. He sold out to the British. If an English spy had not been caught, West Point would have fallen to the enemy. Our brave commander, General Washington, would have been captured."

There were cries and shouts of surprise.

"Not Arnold! Not the hero of the battles of Quebec and Saratoga!"

"You can't mean it, sir," cried Speaker Harrison. "Not one of our most brilliant patriots?"

"Read it for yourself," said the man, dropping the paper onto a table and sinking into a chair.

"Tavern keeper! Ale for this man," called Colonel Marshall.

John picked up the paper and read the story aloud. The plot had been uncovered on September 23, 1780, when a British spy was captured a half mile below Tarrytown, New York. He was carrying secret information given to him by General Arnold.

"Where's Arnold now?" demanded Mr. Henry.

"Free," replied John. "The American officer who held the spy did not realize that General Arnold was involved in the plot. The officer informed the General himself, and Arnold escaped."

The room grew quiet as the men thought about the story of treachery.

"What have we come to when our own men turn against us?" asked Jacquelin Ambler sadly. "I tremble for the fate of our country."

"No, sir," cried Patrick Henry. "We must not tremble. We must not falter, but fight on. We have not heard the last of Benedict Arnold, nor has he heard the last of the men of Virginia!"

A few weeks later, on January 5, 1781, Benedict Arnold, leading British troops, sailed up the James River and landed at Richmond. Military plants were burned. Major Tarleton, who had been terrorizing citizens of Georgia and the Carolinas, rode into the city. Governor Jefferson and the members of the legislature escaped just in time.

The men of Virginia were caught off guard. General Arnold met no resistance.

Now at last Governor Jefferson called upon the militia to act. Captain John Marshall rode at the head of his small band of soldiers. Few in number and armed with their own rifles, the men were led by John south along the James River.

"We'll try to cut off Arnold's retreat below Westover," John told his lieutenant.

"Do we have enough men for that, sir?"

"Probably not," said John grimly. "At least we can give the British some trouble."

That was all that could be expected. John's men fought bravely, but General Arnold's men vastly outnumbered them. It was not long before John was

forced to retreat. It seemed there was no stopping the British there.

Families like the Amblers fled to the homes of relatives in the country. John worried about Polly. Was she safe? Was she frightened?

Units of militia regrouped and fought heroically. General Washington sent an army of men under General Lafayette to help. Finally the British were forced south and back to the sea.

Several months later General Washington trapped the English on the peninsula at Yorktown, Virginia. In October of 1781, General Cornwallis surrendered. The war was over at last!

For months after the victory celebrations, men continued to criticize Governor Jefferson. John Marshall, too, felt that the invasion of Virginia should have been prevented.

"If only Jefferson had allowed us to prepare!" he told his father.

"We cannot blame Mr. Jefferson alone," said Colonel Marshall. "Look at our government. It is weak and hardly efficient."

It was true! All throughout the war the states had been debating a plan of government called the Articles of Confederation. Only recently had all states agreed to it. Under this plan the states could do pretty much as they pleased. No one was really in charge.

"If General Washington had had the authority he needed during the war, he could have ordered Virginia to prepare for an invasion of British troops," Colonel Marshall went on. "As it was, the General could only warn Governor Jefferson of the danger and hope that Jefferson would get his soldiers ready."

"And General Washington hoped in vain," said John. He shook his head. "There is much more to the business of freedom than I thought," he added gloomily.

Colonel Marshall had to laugh at his son's hopeless look.

"Don't laugh, Father," said John. "When all the fighting is done, I see now that it is sound government that protects free men."

"John," said Colonel Marshall, "I think you have a lifelong battle on your hands. Why don't you stand for the legislature? That way you can help make laws that will strengthen our new country. I'm sure our friends in Fauquier County would be happy to have you represent them."

John won the election easily. His neighbors were impressed with his war record and his honesty. Many of John's comrades had recently returned from the army and were eager to support their captain.

John returned to Richmond in the fall of 1782. He was determined to provide good government for his state and his country. But most of all he meant to protect the rights of the family he hoped to have. Polly had promised to become his wife. In January of 1783, they were married.

After the war there was little money in Virginia. John had less than most. His family owned a great deal of land, but that did not make up for the need for ready cash. He and Polly moved into a small, two-room house behind the Ambler home in Richmond.

John took his old law notebook from his William and Mary College days and turned it upside down. On its pages he tried to keep an account of his money. But he was not good at saving. He and Polly were poor, but happy.

The work among Virginia's lawmakers John found discouraging. He tried to propose laws that he felt were fair. Again and again he found himself on the losing side. One of the first questions debated by the legislature concerned debts owed to English merchants from before the war. Should the legislature direct the citizens of Virginia to pay what they owed?

Virginians had been in the habit of buying things on credit from England. They had piled up a mountain of debt. Now many men were trying to use the war as an excuse to ignore these debts.

John thought that Virginia's path was clear. Paying debts was a part of the peace treaty the United States signed with England.

"It is a matter of honor that we pay," John told the legislature.

"You speak of honor, sir!" boomed Patrick Henry. "I, too, believe in honor. When will the *British* honor the terms of our peace treaty? When will *they* remove their troops from the Great Lakes' outposts? When will *they* pay the war damages owed to us?"

Mr. Henry looked at John as though he were a child who did not understand politics.

"No, Mr. Marshall! No state can honor such debts until the British honor theirs."

To John this kind of thinking did not seem honorable. The United States must act in good faith, or the peace treaty would become a worthless paper.

Mr. Henry was a persuasive speaker. Many of the legislators were heavily in debt.

"Why, if I began paying now," John heard one of the men say, "my children's children would still not be able to pay all the money I owe."

The legislature voted in favor of Mr. Henry's plan.

John was terribly disappointed. Just as he predicted, other countries were not eager to make trade agreements with the United States. Business was very bad. It grew harder and harder to make a living.

Soon money in Virginia was so scarce that John's father came to a difficult decision. He had fifteen sons and daughters. It was difficult to provide for all of them.

"I think I can make a better living in Kentucky Territory, John. There's opportunity for new land in Kentucky. I'm going there. But I promise you that I'll come back for the christening of your first child."

In the fall of 1783, Thomas Marshall moved permanently to Kentucky. True to his word, he returned the next year for the christening of John's first son. Polly called the baby Thomas after his paternal grandfather.

"How are things in the legislature?" Colonel Marshall asked his son.

"Pretty much the same," said John unhappily. "You

know, Father, some of the older members act as though I shouldn't have ideas at all."

Thomas Marshall's eyes twinkled with amusement. "You have a serious defect, John."

"What is that?" asked his son.

"Youth!" replied Colonel Marshall. "Wisdom is only expected from older men. Your time will come."

"I doubt it," said John.

At twenty-nine he didn't think he was so very young.

John felt that the men of Virginia had a narrow view of government. They seemed to forget that Virginia was part of a nation. They always put the welfare of their state first.

In the next session of the legislature, John proposed what he thought was an important plan.

"Gentlemen, Virginia must begin to raise money to pay her share of the war debt. Good friends, like France, lent us many thousands of dollars. They should not be kept waiting."

John was not an orator like Patrick Henry. He was not wealthy and influential like George Mason, but he spoke plainly and honestly. "No wonder foreign countries do not wish to trade with a nation that does not honor its debts! We must begin payment at once."

John sat down, and the wealthy master of Gunstan Hall rose slowly to his feet. George Mason was a distinguished-looking man with snow-white hair.

"The debt! The debt There is always the debt!" Mr. Mason sighed with annoyance. "Why, Mr. Marshall, should Virginia make herself poor? Other states refuse to raise their share of the money. Why should we give any?"

John was about to reply when Mr. Mason stopped him.

"No, young man," he said. "Let the other states show they are willing to tax themselves and Virginia will follow."

After a short debate John's plan was defeated.

"I'm fed up with politics," John confessed to one of his friends, James Madison. "The courts are where I can succeed best. I'm going to devote my time to the law."

"Don't do that," begged James. "You're needed here." He was a small, thin young man with earnest, intelligent eyes. He and John worked closely together. But even together, they were not able to sway the older members of the legislature.

John shook his head stubbornly. "No, my mind is made up. Besides, I've been engaged for the biggest case I've ever had," he added excitedly. "It will take all my efforts, which I think are wasted in the legislature."

The Fairfax Land Rights case was a difficult one. It involved seventy-five clients, including George Washington himself. The hearings went on for months. John argued brilliantly, so brilliantly that he won an important decision for his clients.

More than that, John won a reputation for being one of the best lawyers in Richmond. His law practice grew and he began to make money at last. He did not even consider returning to the legislature, but his friends kept him informed of everything that went on.

John heard more and more discouraging news. In the national Congress the states were quarreling among themselves about trade laws. The United States was still not able to pay her debts to the countries who had helped during the Revolution.

"What we need is a stronger plan of government," John told his friends. "The Articles of Confederation do not give Congress enough power. Something must be done soon, or our dream of a free and democratic country will die."

## Chapter 5

# *A Bold New Plan*

By 1786, only five years after the end of the war, John Marshall was one of Richmond's most important men.

On Saturdays, when the weather was fair John met with the Barbecue Club for a day of relaxation. There were games, good food, and good talk. The members were the business and professional men of Richmond. John Marshall was their most enthusiastic member. He was also one of the most prosperous, but he never looked the part.

"Mr. Marshall!" exclaimed Polly one morning before he left. Her tone was disapproving. "I wish you would give some thought to buying new clothes."

John looked down guiltily at his shabby coat, without really seeing the threadbare places. Polly was always after him about his appearance. At least no buttons seemed to be missing today.

"What's wrong with my clothes, Polly?" he asked, honestly puzzled. "They're very comfortable."

Polly sighed. She did not know why her husband failed to take any interest in being stylish.

"Comfort isn't everything," she explained patiently. "Don't you see, your clothes are not suitable for an important lawyer?"

"Oh, now, Polly," said John, kissing her good-by. He put the idea from his mind. He couldn't be bothered about something so unimportant as clothes. He went off to join his friends.

But Polly was not willing to give up the idea of new clothes. John Marshall was rapidly becoming a wealthy man. He could well afford new clothes once in a while. His appearance was a constant embarrassment to Polly. She meant to win her point.

Polly was not the only one who noticed John's

careless way of dressing. The men of Richmond were fond of John Marshall. People said that he was the most popular man in the city, because he treated all men as equals. He was as much at home with the small farmer as with wealthy judges. But there was no doubt about it. John's appearance was deceiving.

When John's younger brother James came to Richmond for a visit, he heard an amusing story about John from a complete stranger. James was still laughing when he got to John's house. Polly served the men tea.

"I hear you nearly lost a fee last week, John," said James, and he began to laugh again.

"Oh, that!" said John, giving Polly an anxious glance. "It might have happened to anyone."

"Not the way I heard it," said James. "It could only have happened to you."

No one was more amused by the story than John himself. Still, he had been hoping that Polly would not hear it.

"Why, whatever could have happened, Mr. Marshall?" asked Polly. She didn't know whether to be amused or concerned. Losing a fee was not amusing, and yet James was laughing.

"Your happy-go-lucky husband, Mrs. Marshall, was recommended to a farmer who was seeking a lawyer. In fact, John was recommended as the best lawyer in the county."

"Oh, now, James!" John interrupted. "Polly would not be interested in all that."

"Of course she's interested," insisted James. He turned to Polly and continued. "Well, the farmer took one look at John and thought someone was playing a joke. 'That fellow?' asked the farmer. 'He doesn't look as though he knows his way around a courtroom. From his appearance I'd say he needed help himself. He looks like a tramp!'

"The man engaged a smartly dressed attorney instead," said James. "Imagine! The fellow took John for a tramp!"

James had to pause because he could not control his laughter. "The very next day, this farmer saw John performing brilliantly in court, as usual. He rushed over and begged John to take the case after all. What do you think of that?"

Only then did James notice the stormy look on Polly's face. She set down her teacup with an exasperated thump.

"Oh, Mr. Marshall, you're impossible!" she cried, and ran from the room in tears.

John closed his eyes and shook his head unhappily. "I knew that story would upset her. But you were bound and determined to tell it. What am I going to do now?"

James was contrite. "I'm sorry, John. I didn't mean to cause trouble."

He eyed his brother's clothes ruefully. Now in his early twenties, James looked very much like John, except for their clothes.

"Perhaps she's right, though," suggested James. "No one could ever accuse you of being well-dressed."

"Perhaps I could order a new suit tomorrow," said John reluctantly.

James agreed that a new suit might help. But he knew John's careless habits. The silver buckles at his knees were often undone. He liked to lounge in a chair. Soon the new suit would look as rumpled as the old one.

The brothers strolled outside into the warm September sunshine. They sat down on a bench under a tree.

"Any word from Mr. Madison?" asked James.

"Not yet," said John. "The mails are slow. Sometimes it takes as long as three weeks to get a letter from Maryland." John sighed. "It seems even longer when you are anxious to know what is happening. Of course, I am thankful that the states finally see the need for a stronger government. But I wish they would get on about the business of making changes."

"If any man can come up with a better plan, that man is James Madison," said James. He was pleased that John's friend had been chosen as one of the men to represent Virginia at the Annapolis Convention.

Unfortunately Mr. Madison had no real opportunity to present a plan. Only five states sent delegates to Annapolis. This was not enough to make changes. A few weeks later James Madison was back in Richmond. John was surprised to find that his friend was not discouraged.

"We'll simply have to try again. A group of us are planning another meeting in Philadelphia in May. Sooner or later we will succeed," Madison told John.

"I wish I had your confidence," said John. "What makes you think more states will be interested this time?"

"The times are changing, John. Our country began with the dream that free and independent men would enjoy equal rights no matter how rich or poor they might be. Now the rich are taking advantage of the poor. The rich tax the small farmers and merchants heavily. How long do you think free men will stand for this?"

In February, 1787, reports reached Virginia of a rebellion of small farmers led by Daniel Shays in Massachusetts. Armed and angry, the men demonstrated outside local government buildings.

"They tried to keep the courts from meeting," announced an astonished judge at the Richmond tavern one evening.

"And they nearly succeeded," added an indignant lawyer. "It's the beginning of a second revolution, I tell you. Who knows where these people may strike next? It could happen in Virginia."

The old judge shook his head. "If men lose respect for the courts, how can democracy succeed?"

"When rich men in state governments make laws that are unfair to small farmers, I'd say there was no democracy," said John.

The other lawyers were surprised.

"What do you mean, Mr. Marshall?" demanded the Judge. "Surely you do not approve such unlawful action." He leaned across the polished wooden table and glared at John.

John gazed back calmly.

"In 1776, we began our fight for justice against the King and an unjust government. Is Mr. Shays' rebellion so much different?"

For a moment the old judge was shocked into silence. The angry look left his eyes. "How soon we forget!" he said at last. "You are right, Mr. Marshall. Responsible citizens must correct this problem before it is too late."

Frightened into action by Shays' Rebellion, the states began to elect delegates to the Philadelphia Convention. No one could now deny the need for an improvement in government.

From the time the Constitutional Convention began in May until it was over in September, no one heard a word about what was going on behind the closed doors of the hall.

"Sentries are posted," John's friend James Monroe reported. "And each man has taken an oath to keep the proceedings secret. I don't like this. Why should there be any need for secrecy? What are the delegates up to?"

Many men were concerned and suspicious. Still, no one knew what was really happening. Many people would have been very angry if they did know.

For the delegates had decided not to follow the instructions of their states. They decided not to revise the Articles of Confederation, but to do away with the old plan altogether.

The Virginia delegation was responsible for presenting a completely new plan of government that had been prepared by James Madison.

John knew little more than anyone else. But when the Convention closed and sent out copies of a new constitution, he was pleased.

Most Virginians knew little about what the Constitution said because they had no opportunity to study it. Many men were against it because three of Virginia's delegates refused to sign it. One of these delegates was Edmund Randolph, the popular young governor. Other people were worried because the Constitution contained no Bill of Rights.

Urged by General Washington himself, John returned to politics in 1781. Once again he became a delegate to Virginia's legislature. Since the days before the Revolutionary War nothing had caused such heated arguments. No sooner did the session begin, then the fight was on. The Constitution had to be approved, or ratified, by nine of the thirteen states.

"I propose that Virginia elect a convention to

approve the Constitution as it stands," said Francis Corbin, of Middlesex County.

Patrick Henry was on his feet at once. "Mr. Chairman, Mr. Corbin's resolution does not allow for changes. There are errors and defects in that paper. I insist that he change his resolution. Virginia will propose amendments or not approve the Constitution at all!"

The debate went on for several days. Neither Mr. Corbin nor Mr. Henry was prepared to give in. At last John came up with a compromise. "Mr. Chairman," he said, "I believe there is some merit in both proposals. But I am not fully satisfied with either. We must not show prejudice. We must not direct the members of our convention to act any particular way. It seems to me the Constitution should be laid before the people for free discussion."

This plan pleased even Patrick Henry. John's resolution was passed. He would have been very happy about this victory, if he had not been so worried about Polly. She was expecting a third child in December. But she had not been at all well.

Three doctors came to see her that fall. No one was able to help very much. The baby was born on December 3. They named this boy Jacquelin, after Polly's father.

Everyone expected Polly to improve, but she did not grow stronger.

"Be patient," advised Dr. Foushee. "These things take time."

John tried his best. Each evening he brought home stories of the day's events.

"What do you think, Polly? I'll be opposing your own doctor for a seat at Virginia's Constitutional Convention. Dr. Foushee is an Anti-Constitutionalist candidate. I'm afraid he has many supporters."

"Dr. Foushee is a good medical man," said Polly. "But no one is so popular as you, John."

John Marshall and Governor Edmund Randolph were the two candidates elected from Henrico County. Polly was right. It was well known that John supported the Constitution. Most people were against it. But John was so popular that he won by a large majority.

James Madison returned from New York just in time to be elected a delegate to the Convention too. "This may be the longest and most difficult battle we have ever had to fight," he told John. "There will be long debates. I'm counting on your help. We must win."

CHAPTER 6

# *What Will Virginia Do?*

JOHN MARSHALL and his younger brother James made their way through the crowded streets of Richmond toward the old Capitol. They paused outside the building and watched delegates arrive. It was the first day of June, 1788. The Virginia Convention was about to meet to debate the new Constitution.

"I wish we could get on with it," cried James. He had recently returned from New York. "What will Virginia do? That's all I've been hearing for weeks. All the states are watching us."

The Constitution had already been approved by eight of the thirteen states. Only nine were needed to turn the new plan of government into law. Would Virginia be that ninth state?

"The battle won't be won or lost on the first day," said John. "Be patient. Time is on our side."

The brothers joined the crowds who watched excitedly as Edmund Pendleton arrived. He was riding in a covered, black phaeton drawn by two white horses. The crowd stared with awe as the crippled old judge was helped from his carriage. The Judge made his way painfully on crutches into the hall. Respectfully, the men touched their hats in silent salute.

"I'm glad Judge Pendleton is on our side," whispered James. "He can influence many votes."

John thought the delegates planned to make the Judge chairman of the Convention. Having a Constitutionalist in that key position would be a great advantage.

A small, one-horse gig drew up, and the crowd broke into loud cheers and applause for Patrick Henry. Stooped and thin, Mr. Henry looked older than his fifty-two years. But when he smiled and waved to his admirers, he seemed to command the crowd.

"He still has the old magic," said John.

"Dangerous magic," said James.

Everyone knew Mr. Henry was decidedly against the new Constitution.

"Do you think he can be persuaded to change his mind?" asked James.

"I doubt it. Mr. Henry is a stubborn man," said John. "I'd best join the other delegates now. If you hurry, you'll find a good seat in the gallery."

Inside, the building swarmed with delegates from every part of Virginia. There were wealthy lawyers, plantation owners, small farmers, and shopkeepers. At one end of the hall, the Kentucky delegation was holding a noisy meeting. As a territory of Virginia, Kentucky had fourteen votes. These delegates were frontiersmen and Indian fighters. They wore fringed buckskin shirts and carried long knives at their belts.

Men from every walk of life had been elected to

consider the new plan of government. Most people agreed that on this first day the Anti-Constitutionalists had enough votes to defeat the Constitution. That meant John would have to work very hard to persuade some of the delegates to change their minds.

Almost as soon as the discussion began, the Anti-Constitutionalists made a serious mistake. George Mason rose and addressed Chairman Pendleton. Although Mr. Mason had helped to write the Constitution, he had refused to sign it because it did not include a Bill of Rights. "I believe the fullest and clearest investigation of this new plan is necessary," said the silver-haired gentleman. "Therefore, I suggest we debate the new Constitution part by part."

John caught James Madison's eye. The two exchanged a look of surprise. Mr. Madison had thought that the opposition would try to frighten the other delegates. He expected them to say that the new Constitution was dangerous. He never thought that they would give anyone a chance to explain each part.

Now, James Madison, as leader of the Constitutionalists, leaped to his feet. He accepted the proposal because this was exactly what he had hoped to do.

A puzzled look crossed George Mason's face. He was not yet aware of his mistake.

John and his friends were delighted with this mistake, but Patrick Henry put the Constitutionalists on the defensive again.

"By what right," asked Mr. Henry, "did the Philadelphia Convention write a constitution at all?"

As everyone knew, the delegates had been elected to

change the Articles of Confederation. Nothing more!

To answer this charge James Madison asked Chairman Pendleton to speak. The choice of speakers at particular times was very important. Mr. Madison had organized his defense of the Constitution carefully. The words of the wise old judge at this time would be carefully weighed by the delegates.

Edmund Pendleton struggled to his feet and stood with the aid of his crutches. "The question we have been elected to debate is not whether the delegates were right in setting forth a new plan of government, but whether or not Virginia is willing to accept that plan," he argued.

Mr. Henry was not easily discouraged. He decided to use another approach. He would discuss the Constitution part by part as had been agreed. He began with the first sentence of the new Constitution. "By what right did the delegates say, 'We the People'? Why not, 'We the States'?"

John saw at once that this was a clever move. One of Virginia's greatest fears was that she would lose her rights as a state. She would be only one of a group of thirteen. How could she be sure her rights would be guarded?

The Kentucky delegation listened carefully to this argument. Loss of states' rights could mean loss of the Mississippi. The Northern states did not depend on this river for transportation. The North might outvote the South and bargain the Mississippi away to another country like Spain or England. Kentucky delegates were not at all sure that the North would have the

South's best interests at heart. Mr. Henry played skillfully upon this fear whenever he could.

The Constitutionalists were worried. Mr. Henry seemed to have scored an important victory. Drastic action was necessary. James Madison decided to take the Convention by surprise. The next speaker he had ready was the young and handsome governor, Edmund Randolph.

When the Governor rose to speak, Patrick Henry and George Mason relaxed. Governor Randolph, like George Mason, had refused to sign the Constitution. He was on their side.

To everyone's amazement, the Governor announced a change of heart. "I would rather cut off my right arm than harm my country," he said. "I am now convinced that it is too late to make changes in the Constitution without harming our country."

The Governor urged the delegates to vote for approval of the Constitution. His words had the force of an explosive.

George Mason half rose from his chair, his face red with fury. "Traitor! Look at young Arnold!" he cried, comparing the Governor to Benedict Arnold.

There was an excited murmuring in the gallery. Such insulting words might mean a duel. But Governor Randolph seemed to take no notice of them. He went on with his speech, answering Mr. Henry's argument. "Why not 'We the People'?" he asked. "The government is for the people. They will elect their representatives, not the states."

James Madison spoke next. Because Mr. Madison

was not a tall man, he could not be seen by everyone. His voice was so low, the delegates could not always hear him. He stood with his hat in his hand, often glancing inside it. There he kept his notes. His calm, logical approach made sense, but few people heard him.

On the other hand, when Mr. Henry spoke of the dangers of a strong national government, people could almost feel the chains binding their wrists. Mr. Henry was easily seen and heard by everyone. He gestured dramatically with his long arms. His voice thundered through the hall.

Whenever Mr. Henry spoke, the galleries were packed. People deserted the Jockey Club races to cheer and applaud him.

For two weeks the Constitution was debated, part by part. It was impossible to tell which side held the advantage. Neither seemed to hold it for long.

During this time James Madison did not call upon John Marshall to speak. But at the beginning of the third week, Mr. Madison decided that John must answer Captain James Monroe's remarks. Even old friends found themselves on opposite sides in this battle.

Captain Monroe was the first of the Revolutionary War veterans to speak. He was against the Constitution.

"What is this wild haste? Why must we be in such a hurry to overthrow our old government for a dangerous new one?" James Monroe asked.

At thirty-three John Marshall, like James Monroe,

was one of the younger members of the convention. He, too, was a Revolutionary War veteran. He had many friends in the galleries and among the delegates. They liked his friendly manner and the simple terms in which he explained the ideas of the new government, which so few people understood.

For his first important speech John wore a new blue coat that Polly had insisted he should buy. He felt a little uncomfortable in it, but when he looked around and saw his friends, John relaxed. He talked to them as he would if he met them on the street, or in his home. "We, the friends of the new Constitution, prefer it, because, sir, we love democracy. If we felt that the old system could secure our liberty and promote our happiness, we would not be so willing now to part with it."

Mr. Henry and the foes of the Constitution had suggested that the Congress and the President could never be trusted to do the will of the people.

"This cannot be true," said John. "It is the people that give power and can take it back."

He pointed out that the government was dependent upon the free will of the people through elections.

John's explanations were very clear. His popularity was great. Mr. Madison thought it would be wise to call upon the young lawyer a second time. John would have to answer Mr. Henry's arguments about the court system under the new plan.

Patrick Henry said that the new system would destroy the rights of the people. Soon, perhaps, there would be no more trial by jury.

"The purse is gone, the sword is gone, and now the very scales of justice are to be given away," cried Mr. Henry emotionally.

The impact of Mr. Henry's speech could not be measured. He had succeeded in communicating his own fears to the people.

John's task was to calm them. It was a tremendous responsibility. His throat felt dry, and he had difficulty keeping his nervous hands still. But he had planned his arguments carefully. Once he began, their logic gave him courage. "The federal courts are not designed to take over the work of state courts," he said. "Citizens will always have their right to trial by jury. The new courts will deal with cases that might arise under the Constitution. Where can arguments between states be settled now? These new courts would decide such cases."

Then John said something men were to remember in years to come. "The Supreme Court will provide a very important protection. Suppose a law were passed that was not constitutional? The judges of the Supreme Court would declare it not a law," he announced.

In his quiet manner John had shown what a brilliant plan the new Constitution was. It provided for three branches of government. Each branch checked and balanced the others. No one branch could ever gain too much power.

Still, John had not convinced Patrick Henry. On the last day of debate Mr. Henry spoke for eight hours. He warned against the evils of the new plan. Those

delegates who had not made up their minds might have been convinced by Mr. Henry's last speech.

Finally, the delegates began to vote. No one could predict the outcome. It was entirely possible that either side might win or lose by one or two votes.

The ballots were counted. The Constitutionalists waited anxiously for the results of the balloting. It was terribly close. But John and his friends had won by only ten votes. Virginia approved the Constitution!

CHAPTER 7

## *The Mysterious Agents X, Y, and Z*

AS THE BRIG *Grace* slowly sailed down Delaware Bay, John Marshall hurried to his cabin. Before the pilot boat left them, John would just have time to write one more letter to be taken back to shore.

"My dearest Polly," wrote John. "The land is just escaping from my view. . . ."

John was on his way to France. Only a great emergency could have persuaded John to leave his home and family. In July, 1797, there was such an emergency. The United States was in serious trouble. She had not been able to come to an understanding with the new French government. President John Adams was sending John Marshall as one of three special agents to try to make some kind of agreement with the French.

The French people had been inspired by the Americans. They, too, had had a revolution, but a very bloody one. The people had beheaded the French king and queen. Men and women of the nobility were being arrested and put to death without a trial of any kind. The American people were divided. Some agreed with the new President, John Adams, that the Americans should not take sides in this struggle. Others, like Thomas Jefferson, who was now the new Vice-President of the United States, felt sympathy for the French people.

After seven weeks at sea, John's ship landed in Holland, where he met one of the other two agents, Charles Cotesworth Pinckney from South Carolina. General Pinckney brought John to meet Mrs. Pinckney and their little daughter.

John smiled into the little girl's eyes and touched her hair gently.

"How fortunate you are, sir, to have your family with you! We have a little girl, too. We call her Mary. She is nearly two years old," John told them. His voice was heavy with homesickness.

The mission got off to a very slow start. General Pinckney and John Marshall waited in Holland several weeks for Elbridge Gerry, of Massachusetts. He was the third agent. When Mr. Gerry did not come, John and General Pinckney went on to Paris and met Mr. Gerry there.

Mr. Gerry's quick, nervous movements made him appear birdlike.

"We must arrange for a meeting with the Minister of Foreign Affairs, Charles Maurice de Talleyrand. I am sure I can easily do this," Mr. Gerry announced confidently. "Monsieur Talleyrand and I knew one another in Boston."

Talleyrand had plotted for years against the royal French government. He had spent two years of exile in the United States. Since Mr. Gerry and Talleyrand had been friendly at that time, John knew at once that Mr. Gerry's sympathies would probably be with the French.

Mr. Gerry was not able to get an audience with the Foreign Minister in spite of his earlier friendship. When Talleyrand did agree to meet the Americans, it was not in government offices, but in his home.

"How gracious of the Foreign Minister!" said Mr. Gerry.

John Marshall frowned. "On the contrary, Mr. Gerry. How insulting! By refusing to receive us in government offices, Talleyrand is treating the representatives of the United States as unimportant."

General Pinckney agreed with John. "He means to discourage us."

When the Americans met Talleyrand, John thought the Frenchman was the ugliest human being he had ever seen.

At forty-two Marshall was tall, slim, and youthful. Talleyrand, at the very same age, seemed old beyond his years. His eyelids were puffy and his face was pale. His cheeks were bony. He walked with a decided limp, for he had been born with a twisted foot.

"I'm a busy man," Talleyrand told them impatiently. "Allow me to present to you these cards of hospitality. They will protect you from annoying visits from the police."

John raised his dark brows. "Is this customary?"

"My dear Mr. Marshall, you should know that after a revolution one cannot be too careful. There are enemies everywhere," Talleyrand informed him in a harsh, rasping voice.

John wished he could have told the Foreign Minister that the United States did not live under a dictatorship that only pretended to be a democracy. He politely refrained. "You will be informed of what steps will follow," said Talleyrand and dismissed them.

"What did he mean by that?" demanded General Pinckney, as they left.

John shrugged. "Intrigue of some kind. That is a very shrewd man. I don't trust him for a moment."

"Oh, nonsense," said Elbridge Gerry. "Forgive me, gentlemen, but you are both woefully lacking in diplomatic skill. It's part of French policy to move slowly and carefully."

Charles Pinckney squeezed his portly form into their

coach. "An honest man is an honest man!" he exclaimed indignantly. "He speaks out plainly. Talleyrand is a sly fellow. I don't like him."

The three ambassadors soon learned that Talleyrand was also ambitious. He was not only close to the present dictator, Barras, but his influence upon General Napoleon Bonaparte also became apparent. General Bonaparte was rising in popularity. He had succeeded in winning military victories all over Europe. There were rumors that Napoleon meant to march against England.

The weeks in France dragged by. The Americans received no direct message from Talleyrand. But finally they were visited by a mysterious man who identified himself as an agent of the French government, Monsieur Hottenguer. "Ah, Mr. Marshall, I am pleased to meet you," he said. "I have heard much about you."

Hottenguer seemed a pleasant enough fellow, but he soon made it clear that he wanted to see General Pinckney alone. The other two agents remained in an outer room trying to guess what Hottenguer was after.

"Talleyrand sent him," said Mr. Gerry knowingly. "He will let us know what the French government expects of us."

"Couldn't Talleyrand himself do that?" asked John Marshall.

Elbridge Gerry sighed. "As I have said before, Mr. Marshall, you are new to the ways of diplomacy."

John had to agree with that. But when General Pinckney told them that Talleyrand's agent had suggested a bribe as the first step toward understanding, John was furious. "A bribe!"

"Yes, a quarter of a million dollars from the American government," replied General Pinckney, his round face flushed with indignation. "The money would be used by Talleyrand to soothe the feelings of the members of the new French government. They feel that President Adams has been most unfriendly. They are insulted."

"The French are insulted!" cried John Marshall. "What about us? I think this man Hottenguer should be completely ignored. Such a demand is outrageous. It's like blackmail. Where will it end?"

"Exactly!" replied General Pinckney.

"Gentlemen! Gentlemen!" Elbridge Gerry shook his head. "You are wrong. This is merely the French way. Pay the price. The American people are willing to support the French Revolution."

"In the form of a bribe?" asked Marshall. "Never!"

"You misunderstand, I am sure. Why don't we ask Monsieur Hottenguer to put his request in writing?" suggested Mr. Gerry.

General Pinckney was willing to try, but Monsieur Hottenguer refused. "After all, it was only a suggestion," he explained quickly—too quickly, John thought.

"You know, of course, that the request did not come from Talleyrand himself, but from someone very close to him," the French agent went on mysteriously.

"Who?" demanded Charles Pinckney. "Enough of

this secrecy. We wish to deal directly with Talleyrand."

The next evening Monsieur Hottenguer brought another man to John's rooms after dark. The apartment glowed with candlelight as the agent was introduced.

"This is Monsieur Bellamy," Monsieur Hottenguer said. "I will leave you gentlemen to speak privately."

"Ah, America! When I think of your country, gentlemen, I remember with gratitude the generous spirit of your people," said Monsieur Bellamy. His smile was disarming. "Everyone was so kind during my visit there. I am Swiss, you know."

General Pinckney peered at this new visitor suspiciously. "No, we did not know, sir. We thought you could speak for Talleyrand," he added impatiently.

"We thought you could help us find some way to reason with him," added John Marshall smoothly.

Whoever this man was, they must not allow him to see their anger, yet.

Mr. Bellamy spoke with them for nearly two hours. He repeated Monsieur Hottenguer's suggestion of a quarter-of-a-million-dollar bribe.

"This is outrageous," said John after their visitor had gone. "We must no longer allow Talleyrand to think we are considering the payment of bribes suggested by secret agents who may, or may not, be representatives of France. If the Foreign Minister wants money for some specific reason, let him tell us so himself, in his official capacity."

"And in our official capacity, we can refuse if we wish," added General Pinckney.

But Mr. Gerry would not allow them to send any such message to Talleyrand. Instead, Mr. Gerry met privately with the secret agents, and once with Talleyrand himself. But even Mr. Gerry did not succeed in getting the request for money in writing. John was certain then that the request was, indeed, nothing more than a bribe.

John Marshall had been living in cramped quarters for three months. In November it was arranged for the agents to live in the home of a charming rich widow.

Madame de Villette often sat with the Americans in the evening. "We are most proud of our gallant Napoleon," she told them. "He has forced his own terms upon Austria," she chattered gaily. "They say Napoleon's Army is feared everywhere."

"I would like to see this Napoleon," remarked John.

"Oh, Mr. Marshall, you will have the opportunity. Napoleon is returning to France," Madame de Villette informed him.

At the triumphal parade in Napoleon's honor, the American agents did glimpse the heroic military leader.

"He is such a small man!" exclaimed John in surprise.

Madame de Villette raised attractive, dark eyes to his. "But a magnetic man. His soldiers adore him. They will die for him."

The lovely widow tapped John's arm with her closed

fan. "Have a care, Monsieur Marshall! Your country would do well to pay the price asked. When Napoleon marches against England, the British Empire will fall. The United States will fall with it, unless—" she paused.

"Unless?" questioned John.

"Unless she has friends," finished the lady, smiling.

John Marshall did not believe that Americans needed that kind of friend. He was only mildly surprised to find that this lovely woman was, no doubt, another of Talleyrand's secret agents.

The Americans were visited by still another secret

agent, Monsieur Hauteval. "You cannot imagine the trade advantages friendship with France could bring, gentlemen," he said.

"Our instructions are not to take sides. We will trade with England and France alike," said Marshall. "This is what we wish to make clear."

Monsieur Hauteval threw up his hands. "Then your country is doomed, gentlemen. You cannot hope to save yourselves when Britain falls unless you side with France. And America must pay the price in gold."

"No!" cried General Pinckney, losing his temper. "Not a penny!" he shouted.

By March of 1798, nearly a year after their mission began, John Marshall, with the aid of General Pinckney, finally convinced Mr. Gerry that they must put their own terms in writing and send them to Talleyrand.

A month later in April, Talleyrand agreed to see the three Americans. He ignored their terms and demanded money himself.

"No," Marshall told him. "Never can we consider a bribe."

Talleyrand was angry. As soon as the Americans left, he decided on a clever move.

Talleyrand sent a letter to America, which he hoped would fire public opinion against the Federalists and President Adams. In it he said that only Mr. Gerry truly meant to be on friendly terms with France. Marshall and Pinckney were acting against the interests of the American people by stubbornly refusing to come to reasonable terms.

Talleyrand's plan might have succeeded, if President Adams had not received John Marshall's letters first. These were published for the entire nation to read. The President removed the French agents' real names and called them instead X, Y, and Z. The President brought the true story of the attempted bribe to the American people. Everyone was proud of the way John and the other ambassadors had acted.

But when John Marshall landed in New York in June of 1798, he was discouraged. He thought his mission had failed because no treaty with France had been made. He was anxious to get home to Polly and the children. Another baby had been born in January, a boy named John.

John Marshall was not prepared for the crowds that met and cheered him as he rode into Philadelphia to report to the President.

"You're a hero, Mr. Marshall," President Adams told him happily. "Haven't you heard?"

The President laughed aloud to see John's amazement. "You have successfully protected the honor of your country against the evil agents X, Y, and Z."

When John realized the important influence his letters had had on making the people understand the French treachery, he was pleased to have been able to give such a great service to his country. "But it's home for me now," he told the President. "All I want is my quiet house, my beloved family, and my law practice in Virginia."

He sighed. "I doubt that any political position will ever tempt me again."

John Marshall did not know how soon his plans would be challenged by General Washington.

CHAPTER 8

# *The Struggle for Power*

GEORGE WASHINGTON was worried about the future of the Federalist Party. After his two terms as first President of the United States, the General had retired to his home in Virginia. Still, he was perfectly informed about the nation's business.

Now as President Adams began his second year, General Washington asked John Marshall to visit at the beautiful home on the Potomac River. The former President invited his nephew Bushrod Washington and John to take tea on Mount Vernon's columned piazza. Here he revealed his purpose for calling them together. "What we need, gentlemen, is more Federalists in Congress. We cannot allow the Republicans to force us out of government."

John agreed with General Washington. The Federalists believed that a strong central government was the only one that would help the new nation grow and prosper. On the other hand, Thomas Jefferson and his Republicans opposed this idea. They felt that the nation's strength lay in the power of the individual

states. In Congress, the Republicans were constantly voting down Federalist plans.

"What I propose, Mr. Marshall," the General went on, "is that you make plans to run for Congress at once."

John was astonished. "Why, sir, even if I did agree to run for Congress, I don't think I could win. Mr. Jefferson and his Republicans all but control my district in Virginia."

General Washington was not disturbed. He sipped

his tea calmly and nodded to his nephew. Bushrod Washington recognized the signal. He leaned forward and spoke earnestly. "You underestimate your own popularity, Mr. Marshall. Your conduct in France has made you a hero."

"That is a generous compliment. I thank you for it, sir, but we cannot forget Mr. Jefferson's popularity. We cannot forget the damage the Alien and Sedition Acts have done to our Federalist Party," said John.

When the Federalists in Congress passed these laws, John had disapproved strongly. The Alien Act gave the President power to order from the country any foreigner who seemed dangerous. The Sedition Act provided for fine and imprisonment for those who spoke against the Government. Both laws were directed against the French agents who were causing trouble in America. But both laws were contrary to John's understanding of freedom as expressed in the Bill of Rights. The laws ignored the right to free speech and trial by jury.

The laws were extremely unpopular. Because they had been sponsored by the Federalists, the people were now supporting the more democratic ideas of the Jefferson Republican Party.

John Marshall's arguments had little effect on George Washington. He looked as firm and unyielding as ever.

"Someone must repair the damage, Mr. Marshall, or Mr. Jefferson and his party will gain full control of this country," the General warned.

No one loved his country more than John Marshall

did. No one had more respect for General Washington either. Still, John would not give in. "General, you must understand that I have just spent a year away from my family. My wife is in poor health. My law practice has suffered greatly in my absence. Why, duties to my family do not permit me to serve in Congress."

"Duty to your country requires that you do serve," replied the General quietly. "Patriotism sometimes requires great sacrifices, Mr. Marshall."

When John thought of the many personal sacrifices George Washington had made for his country, serving in Congress seemed very little to give.

So it was that in December, 1799, John Marshall found himself walking along the cobblestone streets of the United States capital with his wife beside him. John smiled down at Polly. "Well, Mrs. Marshall, what do you think of Philadelphia?"

Polly looked lovely in her new fur-trimmed cape and bonnet, but her eyes were sad. "It's elegant, Mr. Marshall," she said solemnly. "But it isn't home. I miss the children."

John sighed. "So do I. So do I!" Then his eyes began to twinkle, and he laughed. "Look at us, Polly. Here we are on our way to call on President and Mrs. Adams, and all we can think of is the children. You know, I have the feeling that if young Thomas or Jacquelin had an opportunity to see the President, they would not give a thought to us!"

Polly smiled when she thought of her oldest boys. They were growing so fast. Thomas was fifteen and

Jacquelin was just twelve. "I suspect you're right. I'd best keep my eyes open and notice everything. They'll plague us with questions when we get back. It isn't everyone who is asked to call on the President, is it?" asked Polly.

John thought that it wasn't everybody who was called on to enter politics when all he wanted was the peace and quiet of his home. Politics was not a peaceful business.

The election had been a difficult battle. At first it had looked as though John Marshall did not have a chance. When he announced that he was against the Alien and Sedition Acts, many people did not believe him. "Marshall is going against his own party just to win votes," they said.

If it had not been for Patrick Henry, John Marshall might have lost the election. The Republicans fought him every way they could. Some tried to use the strength of Patrick Henry's voice against Mr. Marshall. This was a mistake, because no one had bothered to consult Mr. Henry. To everyone's surprise Patrick Henry vigorously supported John Marshall.

In a fiery letter Mr. Henry said, "Tell Marshall I love him because he felt and acted as a Republican, as an American, in France."

Without Patrick Henry's letter, Marshall might have lost the election. In the end he won by 108 votes.

John Marshall had been in the House of Representatives only two weeks when it became his duty to make an announcement that saddened the nation.

With tears in his eyes he stood before the House and

spoke in a voice that shook with emotion. "The late President of the United States is no more."

George Washington had died at his home at Mount Vernon. The bells of Philadelphia began their dismal tolling. The business of government stopped. Men wept openly in the streets. The loss was a deeply personal one. It was Washington's determined spirit that had guided them so skillfully through the storm of the revolution and the first, difficult years of the young republic.

The next day John Marshall became the first American to speak of the former President as "first in war, first in peace, and first in the hearts of his countrymen."

The words had been written by Henry Lee, but no one felt them more strongly than John. He read them in a choked voice. Perhaps it helped to know that he had been able to grant his general's last request by taking up the fight for the Federalists in Congress.

Hardly was the period of mourning over when the conflict in the House of Representatives began. John Marshall fought valiantly for the Federalists on every issue, but when the Republicans introduced a bill to repeal the Alien and Sedition Acts, Marshall courageously voted with the Republicans just as he had promised in his campaign.

"That's the end of Marshall's career in politics," said the Republicans. "He calls himself a Federalist, and yet he votes with the Republicans. His own party can't count on his support."

Although many Federalists were angry, John's career

was far from over. President Adams offered John Marshall the position of Secretary of State.

"Secretary of State!" cried Polly, when the letter came. "Oh, Mr. Marshall, that means months and months away from home. When will we be a real family again?"

"We're always a family, no matter where I am," said John. "The appointment will only last a short time, less than a year. Mr. Jefferson is certain to win the next presidential election. I have a feeling he will be quite happy to leave me in Richmond, safely minding my own business."

John did not tell Polly that he did not expect a Federalist would ever be elected President again after John Adams retired.

"There is only one way the Federalists can hold onto power in the government," President Adams told John Marshall.

"What did you have in mind?" asked Marshall.

The President led him into a private office and asked him to sit down.

"Let me tell you my plan," said the President. "It is true that Mr. Jefferson and the Republicans control Congress. But what of the courts, Mr. Marshall? So far no Republican has been appointed a federal judge. I do not intend to name any myself."

"But surely once Mr. Jefferson is in office he will name some," protested Marshall.

President Adams held up his hand. "Before I leave office the Federalists in Congress must pass a law to enlarge the court system. Then I will appoint more

Federalists to the new posts. These appointments cannot be changed by the new President. No, Mr. Marshall, the Federalists will control the courts."

John Marshall was impressed by President Adams' plan. The law was quickly passed. Just as quickly, President Adams began to fill these new posts with Federalist judges. The balance of power was preserved.

The summer of 1800 was a difficult one for John Marshall. He could not spend his time relaxing with his family at Oak Hill. Instead, President Adams had asked him to go to the new capital that was being built in Washington, D.C.

It was a hot, uncomfortable place to be. Most of the government buildings were unfinished. The rest of the city looked like a frontier town with frame houses and muddy roads.

President Adams hurried off to Massachusetts at the beginning of the summer. His wife was gravely ill. Vice-President Jefferson was at his home in Monticello. John Marshall was left to see to the nation's affairs. That summer he was acting President of the United States.

In the fall he made a brief visit home. But in December he was back for the session of Congress. President Adams was still busy appointing new judges. Secretary of State Marshall was equally busy writing out commissions for the positions.

Early in January, President Adams received unexpected news. Oliver Ellsworth, Chief Justice of the Supreme Court, had resigned because of poor health.

"Perhaps Mr. Jay would take his old position back," said President Adams thoughtfully. "He's a strong man and a good Federalist."

John Jay had been the first Chief Justice of the Supreme Court. He had resigned in 1795 to become Governor of New York.

Governor Jay politely refused the offer. He did not feel the Supreme Court would ever become very important.

President Adams sent for John Marshall. The President paced up and down his office restlessly. Finally he stopped before John. "Mr. Marshall, I don't know what to do. This is the most important position we Federalists have open to us. A Supreme Court justice is appointed for life."

The President paused. His round face was flushed as he peered up at the Secretary of State. "For life, Mr. Marshall," he repeated. "Do you realize what that means? Think how long the Federalist Party can remain in control of the Supreme Court! Whom can I nominate to such an important position?"

John Marshall did not know what to say. "Surely, Mr. President, there are many good men about."

President Adams shook his head. "I've studied list after list of recommendations."

The President seemed uncomfortable. He adjusted the fine lace at his cuffs and brushed a tiny speck of dust off the sleeve of his handsome coat. At last he met John Marshall's gaze. "No, Mr. Marshall, I think I shall have to appoint you. In fact, I have already sent your name to the Senate. Will you accept?"

"Me?" Secretary Marshall was both pleased and surprised. He had not dreamed such an honor would come to him.

He took a week to think over the offer. He must consider the time he would have to spend away from home. Then, too, the Chief Justice was paid only a small salary. On the other hand, here was the opportunity to help direct the affairs of the United States and keep it strong.

The first two Chief Justices had done little to exert power. John felt that the Supreme Court could be as powerful as the Presidency. He was convinced that the Court could influence the growth of the nation.

Accepting this position would mean sacrifice for John and his family. For a moment he remembered General Washington's words. *Patriotism sometimes requires great sacrifices, Mr. Marshall,* General Washington had said.

On February 4, 1801, John Marshall wrote to President Adams and formally accepted the position of Chief Justice of the United States Supreme Court.

Hardly anyone noticed. In Washington everyone was talking about the presidential election. Mr. Jefferson had not been elected. The result of the electoral vote was a tie. There were 73 votes each for Thomas Jefferson, of Virginia, and Aaron Burr, of New York, both Republicans.

After six days of balloting, the House of Representatives elected Mr. Jefferson President and Mr. Burr Vice-President. It was the middle of February, and the new President was to take office on March 4.

"We've so little time left," mourned President Adams.

He appointed judges and had them approved as quickly as possible. John Marshall, who had held the positions both of Chief Justice and of Secretary of State these last few weeks, signed commissions rapidly. He worked until nine o'clock on the evening of March 3. Then, feeling tired, he left the completed commissions on his desk.

I'll have them delivered tomorrow, he thought as he returned to his boardinghouse.

He did not realize that tomorrow would be too late.

## Chapter 9

# *A Clever Decision*

On March 4, 1801, John Marshall hurried from his boardinghouse in Washington to the Senate chamber. There he dressed in the black robe he wore as Chief Justice of the Supreme Court. At noon Chief Justice Marshall offered a Bible to his cousin Thomas Jefferson.

The tall, red-haired Virginian placed his hand firmly on the cover. In a low voice Mr. Jefferson repeated the Presidential Oath of Office after the Chief Justice, "I do solemnly swear that I will faithfully execute the office of President of the United States, and will, to the best of my ability, preserve, protect, and defend the Constitution of the United States."

Everyone listened carefully to the new President's speech afterward. How would the first Republican President feel toward the defeated Federalists?

"President Jefferson was wise to suggest that Americans set aside their differences and try to work together," John Marshall told his brother later.

"He did sound peaceful enough," agreed James. "But it must be very uncomfortable for President

Jefferson to have to work with all the Federalists John Adams appointed to the courts. You will have to be very careful, John. People are saying that the President would like very much to appoint a Republican in your place. Some say he will not give up until he succeeds."

His brother laughed. "You forget. The Chief Justice of the Supreme Court is appointed for life. If anyone asks, I hope you will tell them that John Marshall is in good health and looking forward to a long life."

"It's no joking matter," said James.

Not long after, John Marshall returned to Richmond for a visit. James wrote his brother a letter from Washington. "President Jefferson is angry. John Adams appointed twenty-five Justices of the Peace for the District of Columbia alone. Jefferson thinks eight justices are enough. The fact is, Secretary of State James Madison has not delivered seventeen of the commissions you signed for President Adams."

John felt terribly guilty. He had left those very commissions on his desk the night before the inauguration. Naturally, he assumed the next Secretary of State would deliver them.

The position of Justice of the Peace was not a terribly important one. Most of the disappointed men did not complain. But William Marbury and three other men appealed to the Supreme Court. They were determined to challenge the new President. They insisted upon being given their commissions. This would be the first big problem John and the Court must face. It was not long before the six Justices met to discuss the problem.

The designers of the new capital city had provided a splendid home for the President. The Senate and House of Representatives had handsome chambers. No place had been set aside for the Supreme Court. It met in the basement of the Capitol.

"I feel rather like a poor relation," remarked Justice Bushrod Washington.

Sixty-nine-year-old Justice William Cushing settled himself in a wooden armchair. He removed his spectacles and rubbed the bridge of his long, thin nose. "You are young, Justice Washington. You may even live long enough to enjoy some improvement in our situation. I do not expect to myself. The Supreme Court has done little to justify more attention and respect than it has received."

"Come, come, man," blustered Justice Samuel Chase impatiently. "That's no way to talk. The Court has had little opportunity to exert its influence. Now, with the appeal from Mr. Marbury, perhaps the Court can put these Republicans in their place!" cried the sixty-year-old Justice.

His round face flushed with anger. "The Court can issue a writ of mandamus forcing Secretary Madison to deliver the commissions. And there isn't a thing Madison or Jefferson can do about it."

Justice Chase had been a signer of the Declaration of Independence. He was known for his temper and outspoken manner.

Justice William Paterson looked up from the papers he was neatly sorting on the table in front of him. "Of course, they might just ignore a writ," suggested the scholarly judge.

"Ignore it!" Justice Chase's voice boomed. "They wouldn't dare!"

"They might," said Justice Alfred Moore. He turned to the new Chief Justice. "How could the Court enforce its decision?"

John Marshall leaned back in his chair and clasped his hands behind his head. His dark eyes were thoughtful. "The Court would be powerless. The Secretary of State and the President know this only too well. It may be they are even delighted the case has come up at all."

Bushrod Washington was alarmed. "Then the situation is hopeless. The Supreme Court cannot very well ignore the case. The people will be convinced we are afraid."

"We're doomed no matter what we do," said Justice Paterson gloomily.

"That's the way it looks now," said the Chief Justice. "Perhaps, though, by the time the case comes before us, we can find another way."

During the first sessions of the Court that June and December of 1801, Marshall made a change that seemed to add to the Court's strength. Instead of having each justice read his decision on each case that came before them, Marshall read the Supreme Court decisions himself. In this way Chief Justice John Marshall became the voice of the Court.

In January, 1802, the Republican Congress abolished the Judiciary Law that the Federalists had passed to create new positions for judges.

"That's one way to get rid of unwanted Federalists," remarked Bushrod Washington. "Merely get rid of their jobs. There is even talk of impeaching Justice Chase for his outspoken manner in court. If President Jefferson succeeds, Justice Chase will be forced to resign. After that no justice will be safe."

"Justice Chase has a quick temper," said Marshall. "But I don't think there are real grounds for impeaching him."

"The *Washington Federalist* does," said Bushrod, indicating the newspaper. "It even suggests that Congress will come up with a law to abolish the Supreme Court."

Congress did not go quite that far. It did reduce

Supreme Court sessions to one a year. This put off the next session until after 1802.

"There is one advantage to this," said Marshall. "We will have more time to come up with a solution to the *Marbury* v. *Madison* case."

"Time, yes," said General Washington's nephew. "But not free time. We'll be riding circuit again and involved in more cases than ever."

With the positions of new circuit judges abolished, Justices of the Supreme Court had to take on these duties themselves. They were forced to travel from place to place and act as judges in federal courts that met in the states. John Marshall's circuit included Richmond and extended to South Carolina.

Travel was difficult and tiring, especially for the older justices. Even John Marshall's journeys were not without problems. As usual he tried to see the humorous side.

John wrote Polly from Raleigh, North Carolina, that when he arrived he found that fifteen silver dollars had slipped through his waistcoat pocket and been lost.

Worse than that was the surprise he found when he looked over his unpacked clothes.

"Where are my trousers?" he asked his Negro servant. "I must get dressed for Court."

"Trousers?" said the young man vaguely. "Trousers? I thought I saw them somewhere." He began sorting through the clothes.

While John waited, he looked down at his mud-splattered riding breeches. He knew Polly would never approve of them.

"Have you found the trousers yet?" he asked anxiously.

"Why, sir, I could have sworn they were here," said the servant, scratching his head and looking puzzled. Then he brightened. "We can have some made. Yes, sir! That's it. I'll find us a tailor."

"To make a pair of trousers in less than an hour?" John shook his head ruefully and then shrugged. After all, were clothes really so important?

John Marshall slipped his black robe around his shoulders. The long folds almost covered his riding breeches. They may not have been appropriate attire for Court, but they were better than no trousers at all. "Perhaps no one will notice," he said doubtfully.

The Chief Justice made his appearance. Of course, many people did notice his unusual manner of dress and were shocked. Marshall was merely amused. He enjoyed telling the story afterward, but not to Polly.

The case of *Marbury* v. *Madison* was constantly on the Chief Justice's mind. If the Supreme Court were to survive, it must be strong and independent. It would never do to admit that in this situation the Court was powerless. Together the six justices explored all possibilities.

More than a year after its last session, the Court met in February, 1803. The basement chambers of the Supreme Court were packed with visitors during the proceedings. The black-robed justices sat in a row of high-back, wooden chairs. Their sober expressions hid their feelings as they listened to lawyers argue the case.

Marshall was especially interested in the testimony of the Attorney General, Levi Lincoln.

"Whatever did happen to Mr. Marbury's commission for Justice of the Peace?" one of the lawyers asked.

Either the new Attorney General or the Secretary of State should have found the commissions John Marshall had signed and left on his desk.

"I refuse to answer on the grounds that my testimony might tend to incriminate me," said Attorney General Lincoln.

Marshall rather expected this answer. Probably Mr. Lincoln had illegally burned the commissions. But no one could prove this unless the Attorney General admitted his own guilt. And the Constitution clearly said that no man could be forced to give evidence against himself.

When all the arguments had been heard, it became apparent that the Court must order the Secretary of State to give William Marbury his commission. In doing so, they would put themselves in a very awkward position. How could they force James Madison to do this, if President Jefferson refused to cooperate? Who could force the President to do anything?

John Marshall's decision was a surprise to everyone. He found a clever way out of the dilemma.

In reading the Court's decision, the Chief Justice spent an hour and a half explaining that Mr. Marbury and the three other men were entitled to their commissions.

"Secretary Madison should be asked to deliver them," he said.

"But," the Chief Justice went on, "if Mr. Marbury wishes such an order to be given, he must go to another court. The Supreme Court cannot issue the order. It is not in our power to issue a writ of mandamus in this case."

Amazed, the spectators leaned forward to catch every word. Why, they wondered, couldn't the Supreme Court issue a writ of mandamus in this case? Why couldn't the Court rule that the Secretary of

State abide by the law? In 1789, the Federalist Congress had passed a National Judiciary Act, giving the Supreme Court the power to do just this.

"Congress was wrong," said the Chief Justice. "It was not in the power of Congress to make such a law. The Constitution clearly states the powers of the Supreme Court. The Court has the power to issue a writ of mandamus in only certain very specific cases. Nothing can change that except a change in or an amendment to the Constitution."

The Chief Justice paused and half smiled. "That means," he said slowly, "that the law Congress made in 1789 was unconstitutional!"

Marshall finished reading his long decision. His sharp glance met that of Attorney General Levi Lincoln. Even the Attorney General had to admire the Chief Justice's logic.

"A law in conflict with the Constitution is not a law," declared Chief Justice John Marshall.

James Madison was impressed. Although they were no longer close friends, Mr. Madison had to admire the Chief Justice's skillfull interpretation of the Constitution James Madison had helped write.

"The case has not destroyed the Supreme Court," James Madison told President Jefferson. "John Marshall has found a way to strengthen the Court. If he is going to declare laws unconstitutional, he will be more powerful than ever."

Now President Jefferson considered John Marshall an enemy. If any grounds could be found for impeaching the Chief Justice, President Jefferson would not hesitate to use them. The one thing President Jefferson wanted was to force John Marshall to leave the Supreme Court.

CHAPTER 10

# *The Strange Case of Aaron Burr*

MARKETING in Richmond was usually done by the men of the family. Whenever Chief Justice John Marshall was at home, he liked to go marketing. He would leave the house early in the morning and walk to the city's food stalls. Here he joined his neighbors who bargained with the shopkeepers for fresh fruits and vegetables.

John's oldest son, Thomas, did not approve of this at all. Recently Thomas had been graduated from Princeton University in New Jersey. He was very conscious of appearances. "It isn't dignified, Father," he protested. "Let me go, or Jacquelin."

"Nonsense!" said John. "My friends are used to seeing me at market. Being Chief Justice hasn't changed the fact that I'm the head of a large family. Would you have our friends think that the Chief Justice's family is too dignified to eat?"

John always set off for town in his oldest, most comfortable clothes. His shopping basket hung over his arm and his hat was always pushed back carelessly. He had a ready smile and a pleasant word for the many people who greeted him. They would ask about Polly and the children.

There were six children now. Two more sons had been born since John had returned from France. James was six and a half, and the youngest, Edward Carrington, was only a year and a half old.

Sometimes Polly grew impatient waiting for John to return from market. Shopping seemed to take him twice as long as anyone else because of all the time he spent visiting along the way.

Not everyone recognized the Chief Justice. Strangers to Richmond sometimes took him for a rather poorly dressed servant. One day a man who had just purchased a goose stopped John. "Look here, my man, I'll give you this coin if you'll carry my package and deliver it."

John repressed a grin as he thought of what Polly would say. He shifted his own packages and found he could carry the goose as well.

"Just put it under my arm," said John, who started up the hill.

The man followed along behind. He was surprised at the number of people who greeted John. But he never suspected that he had hired the Chief Justice of the Supreme Court to carry his goose until someone stopped to tell him.

By this time, John's long strides had taken him far ahead. The long neck of the goose hung down and bumped his leg as he walked. The stranger hurried to overtake the Chief Justice.

"Oh, sir! A thousand apologies! If I had only

known—" he sputtered, reaching for the goose. "Won't you let me help you with your packages? To think I hired the Chief Justice as a— as a—"

John's hearty laugh relieved the man's embarrassment.

"No harm done, sir," said John. "We were both going the same way. But, if it's all the same to you, I'll keep the tip."

Those who witnessed the incident spread the story of their good-natured neighbor all over Richmond. John Marshall's friends felt deep affection for him, although they did not always agree with his decisions in Court.

In December of 1806, Marshall returned to Washington. Here, he first learned about the case that would put a severe strain on his friendships.

President Jefferson had uncovered a terrible secret. "I have information that there is a plan to divide our nation," he told Congress. "Evil men are encouraging Western settlers to join them."

It was not until two weeks later that Mr. Jefferson revealed the name of the leader of these men.

"Aaron Burr," announced the President, "is guilty beyond any doubt of high treason. He is a traitor to his country."

"Aaron Burr! The former Vice-President!"

Many people were astonished. Others, like Chief Justice Marshall, had been hearing rumors of Mr. Burr's activities in the Western lands. Marshall's relatives in Kentucky kept him informed.

Soon newspapers carried Mr. Burr's story. While Vice-President of the United States, Aaron Burr had fought a duel with Alexander Hamilton. Mr. Burr was certain that Mr. Hamilton had prevented him from becoming Governor of New York. In the duel, Mr. Hamilton was shot and killed.

When Mr. Burr left his position as Vice-President at the end of President Jefferson's first term, many thought Mr. Burr was ruined. Now it seemed that he had planned to set up an empire in the West. It was said that he had approached the British ambassador for money to help him. He had even spoken to representatives of New England states. It was rumored that Mr. Burr hoped these states would break away from the Union.

If Mr. Burr really planned to make war against the United States, he would need money and arms. There was some evidence that he had tried to find both.

"Mr. Burr is a dangerous criminal," President Jefferson told his friends. "He must be brought to trial and convicted of treason."

The President was so concerned for the safety of the country that he did not stop to consider Mr. Burr's rights as an American citizen.

"Every man has a right to a fair trial," insisted John Marshall. "No one, not even the President, has the right to condemn a man before he has been proven guilty by a court of law."

Marshall's position was not popular. To most people Aaron Burr was a villain. It seemed as though the Chief Justice was protecting a criminal.

As time for the trial grew near, some of John's old friends refused to speak to him. Newspapers in many parts of the country printed editorials that called for the impeachment of Chief Justice Marshall.

The trial of Aaron Burr was to take place in Richmond. John Marshall himself would preside as circuit judge.

Feeling against John was so strong that Polly became ill with worry. "There's talk that your life may be in danger," she cried hysterically.

John tried to calm her. "Now, Polly, that's a terrible exaggeration. The worst that can happen is impeachment. They tried to get rid of Justice Chase that way and failed. No one is going to get rid of me so easily either. Besides, it is my duty to see that Mr. Burr does receive a fair trial. What happens in the courtroom here in Richmond may affect justice in the United States for years to come. We must have courage."

Mr. Burr was brought to Richmond in March of 1807 in the custody of military men. He had been poorly treated. From the time he was captured, he had been forced to travel more than a thousand miles in the same filthy clothes. John immediately had the prisoner transferred to a room at the Eagle Tavern. Here he was kept under guard and given decent clothes and food.

"No prisoner should have to suffer such indignity," said John Marshall.

At the close of the first hearings, the Chief Justice ruled that Mr. Burr could not be held on a charge of treason. Instead, he agreed to a lesser charge of high misdemeanor. Mr. Burr was set free on $10,000 bail.

"The Government," announced Chief Justice Marshall, "has not produced enough evidence to prove treason."

The country was in an uproar. The President said Aaron Burr was guilty of treason. The Chief Justice set him free on bail.

In Washington, President Jefferson and Secretary of State Madison were organizing a search for witnesses to prove Mr. Burr's guilt.

"We will spare no expense," said President Jefferson. "Aaron Burr must be convicted. If John Marshall wants evidence, we will find it."

In Richmond the people were furious with John

Marshall. They called him names in the streets. Sometimes they gathered in front of the large Marshall house and shouted insults.

"Traitor! Power-mad traitor!"

John Marshall simply closed the doors and windows and ignored them. No matter what happened, he meant to give Mr. Burr a fair trial.

The city was crowded with visitors. Most men were convinced of Mr. Burr's treason. But on the street corners one tall young man gave impassioned speeches at all hours of the day and night. He was General Andrew Jackson, of Tennessee. He told of the danger of Spanish attack in the Southwest. "Aaron Burr is no traitor," he said. "He's a hero. He saw the Spanish

making ready to attack our Western frontier. He wanted to lead an army against the Spanish to protect our settlers. Is this treason?"

In May there was a Grand Jury hearing. The Jury would decide whether or not there was now enough evidence to put Aaron Burr on trial for treason. Until this time the exact meaning of treason had not been clear to everyone, so John, as presiding judge, explained it. "According to our Constitution, treason consists of an actual act of war against the United States. Nothing less."

At this time the star witness for the prosecution arrived in Richmond. He was General James Wilkinson, Commanding General of the United States Army at New Orleans. He was the highest-ranking Army officer in the United States.

"Yes, Mr. Burr was organizing an army to march against the Spanish," testified General Wilkinson. "But first that army was to attack American settlements along the frontier territory. That same army was to capture lands belonging to the State of Virginia. Mr. Burr planned to organize his troops on an island in the Ohio River belonging to a Mr. Blennerhassett."

Standing proudly before the jury, General Wilkinson impressed the spectators who packed the Virginia House of Delegates. In his full-dress uniform he was the very picture of American strength and patriotism.

"Mr. Burr sent me messages detailing his plans. I, of course, sent these to President Jefferson," the General announced virtuously.

After four days of cross-examination by the defense

lawyers and Mr. Burr, General Wilkinson appeared less sure of himself. In the end he was forced to admit that he had made some slight changes in the messages. He had erased a word here and there.

The question was, Why?

Compared to General Wilkinson, Mr. Burr was small and very ordinary in appearance. But he did possess great personal courage. Under Mr. Burr's steady gaze, General Wilkinson began to wilt.

Perhaps the General remembered the hours he had spent with Mr. Burr planning a possible attack on the Spanish. For he, too, had been involved in the plot. He said he had only pretended interest to gain information for the good of his country. For some reason, General Wilkinson seemed considerably shaken.

But his testimony was successful. Mr. Burr was indicted for treason. Now Aaron Burr was imprisoned until the trial, which began in the heat of August.

Once again John Marshall cautioned the court. "Treason, according to our Constitution, consists of an act of war against the United States. This is what must be proved."

"The prosecution will prove that Mr. Burr gathered a small army on Blennerhassett's Island in the Ohio River on December 13, 1806," stated President Jefferson's attorneys.

But no witness could be found who actually saw an army gathered on that island. The fact was that when the local militia raided the island, they found nothing but Mr. Blennerhassett's empty house. Many witnesses claimed to have heard Mr. Burr speak of dividing the nation. No one could prove he had actually tried to do so.

At last the defense attorneys protested: "It is improper to hear further testimony about something that never happened."

John Marshall allowed the lawyers to debate the point. The attorneys for the prosecution were angry. They insisted that all their witnesses should be heard. They had more than a hundred men ready. They even hinted that if Marshall ruled against them, he would be impeached by Congress and forced to give up his position as Chief Justice.

John Marshall refused to be frightened by these threats. Finally, he read his decision. It was fifty pages long. "Two witnesses must testify to the actual act of levying war against the United States. Since no witnesses can testify to the presence of Mr. Burr at Blennerhassett's Island with an army, treason cannot be proved."

It was a courageous decision. The Chief Justice knew very well that President Jefferson would be angry when he learned that Mr. Burr had not been convicted. Everyone expected the President to move against Marshall at any moment.

To the loyal friends who admired his honesty, John Marshall was a great hero. In the face of tremendous pressures he had protected the right of an American citizen to a fair trial. But in Baltimore the people sided with President Jefferson. The mock figures of John Marshall and of Aaron Burr were burned in public.

Marshall and his family escaped the angry public and spent several weeks at Oak Hill, their country home.

Although he had not been convicted of treason, Aaron Burr lost the respect of his countrymen. He never rose to a position of power again.

In time the threat of another war with England pushed the strange case of Aaron Burr from the minds of the people. It also drew President Jefferson's attention away from the Chief Justice of the Supreme Court.

CHAPTER 11

# *The Voice of the Court*

TWICE A YEAR, for seven or eight weeks at a time, one of the boardinghouses in Washington was crowded with lawyers and judges. Here the Justices of the Supreme Court stayed while Court was in session. Here, too, stayed the lawyers who were arguing cases before the Court.

Chief Justice Marshall presided over the long dinner table, as he did over the Court. His charm made the boardinghouse a pleasant home for these men.

"I love his laugh," said young Joseph Story enthusiastically.

In 1810, thirty-year-old Mr. Story returned to Washington to argue a case before the Supreme Court and made a favorable impression as a brilliant lawyer.

At that time only two of the original members of John Marshall's first Court were left. Some had died. Others retired. The Court had to be enlarged to seven men because of the growing population in Kentucky, Tennessee, and Ohio.

President Jefferson had managed to appoint men as Justices whom he thought were political friends. He advised the new President, James Madison, on appointments as well.

"Why not appoint young Joseph Story to the Supreme Court?" suggested Thomas Jefferson. "He's a strong Republican. Marshall and Bushrod Washington will then be completely outnumbered by Republicans. Young Story is strong-minded. Marshall will never be able to influence him."

But Mr. Jefferson was wrong. John Marshall's sound logic and his personal charm were so great that the Justices seldom disagreed with the Chief Justice's legal opinions. As for Mr. Justice Story, he soon became the Chief Justice's greatest admirer.

"Why, I believe I am in love with his character," the young Justice wrote to his friend. "He is as patient and agreeable off the bench as he is on."

Once a week the Justices met in a room in the capitol. They spent long hours discussing cases. They even had their meals sent in. The Justices agreed that no wine should be served on these occasions because they wanted to be able to think very clearly. There was one exception. In damp weather a glass of wine was permitted to prevent colds.

But there were times during a particularly difficult meeting that John Marshall would look to Justice Story. "Would you go to the window, sir," he would ask, "and see if there is any sign of rain?"

When Justice Story reported that there was none, a mischievous gleam would light the Chief Justice's dark eyes. "Ah, Justice Story, the powers of the Supreme Court cover a very large territory. It is certain to be raining somewhere. Would you send for some wine to brighten our spirits? It has been a long, hard day."

John Marshall was Chief Justice of the United States Supreme Court for thirty-four years. During that time the Marshall Court handed down many decisions that shaped the new nation and made it strong.

1. The *Marbury* v. *Madison* case established the right of the Supreme Court to declare a law made by Congress unconstitutional and not a law at all.

2. The *Dartmouth College* v. *Woodward* case established the fact that contracts were binding. Businessmen were most pleased by this decision. Be-

cause of this, American business grew and prospered.

3. The *McCullough* v. *Maryland* case established the right of the United States Government to set up federal banks, just as the states were able to set up banks. Most important of all, this case established the fact that the Founding Fathers who had written the Constitution were not able to foresee everything the United States would need and that there were *implied* or suggested powers in the Constitution. The National Banks became very important for business.

But even the Supreme Court could not keep the United States out of war. In 1812, under President James Madison, America once again went to war against Great Britain. It was a bitter conflict. The British succeeded in invading Washington and burning many of the government buildings. But the United States recovered quickly and rebuilt the capital. The new quarters for the Supreme Court were completed after the United States victory.

"You know, John, Justice Cushing was right," Bushrod Washington confided, as he viewed their new, handsome, and spacious surroundings in the Capitol.

"What do you mean?" asked John Marshall. He was settled comfortably in his new leather chair.

Justice Washington smiled. "The very first time we met in our old quarters Justice Cushing suggested that I might live long enough to see our conditions improve. I only wish he were here now to appreciate it."

Justice Washington enjoyed the luxury of pacing about the large quarters. "Do you realize how different things really are? Why, almost every day the Court is in session visitors fill the place. Doesn't the number of lady spectators seem remarkable to you? I think they come to see you, John, the man who made the Supreme Court the strong branch of government that it is today."

"Nonsense, Bushrod!" John Marshall's eyes twinkled. "I rather think the ladies come to see the handsome young lawyers who argue so passionately before us. The ladies are not interested in the old Chief Justice."

But Bushrod Washington knew just how handsome the gray-haired Chief Justice looked. Bushrod only smiled and kept his thoughts to himself.

It was certainly true that Supreme Court cases received much attention from everyone. Brilliant lawyers came from every part of the country to appeal to the Supreme Court. Chief Justice Marshall's final decisions were now so important that lawyers learned to study these cases, as well as his pronouncements, with great care. These decisions often strongly affected legal thinking.

Some cases took years to reach the Supreme Court. One case, known as *Gibbons* v. *Ogden*, began as far back as 1807 and did not reach the Supreme Court until the last year of President James Monroe's administration. That was more than seventeen years later.

The case involved river transport. Robert Fulton

was an inventor, but his partner Robert R. Livingston was a shrewd businessman. Few people realized the effect the steamboat enterprises would have on the United States when the invention was first made known.

"Why, we can make a fortune by controlling all the waterways in New York State," Livingston told the inventor.

"Controlling the waterways? How?" asked Mr. Fulton.

"Leave it to me," said Mr. Livingston. "I know the ways of politics."

Mr. Livingston went to Albany. There he convinced the state legislature to give the Fulton-Livingston Company the exclusive right to sail their steamboats on New York waterways. No one else could carry any kind of cargo unless they paid the Fulton-Livingston Company a large fee. The company grew stronger and richer.

But New York State was growing. More and more ships were needed. A few years later new steamboats appeared on New York waters. Some belonged to Mr. Aaron Ogden. Others to Mr. Thomas Gibbons. The Fulton-Livingston Company sent representatives to both men. "We have no real objection to your sailing New York waters," they said, "but you must pay our company for that privilege. We have an exclusive license from the State of New York."

"You mean you have a monopoly," retorted Mr. Gibbons indignantly. "Well, gentlemen, I, too, have a license to sail all the waterways in the United States. My license was issued by the United States Government. I won't pay you a cent."

Mr. Ogden also had a federal license, but he did not seem to want any trouble. "What is the fee?" he asked and paid at once.

Mr. Gibbons was angry. He tried to carry on his ferrying business, but the Fulton-Livingston Company kept interfering. "Be reasonable, man," the representatives argued. "Ogden has paid the price."

"I'll take the case to the Supreme Court before I pay anything," Mr. Gibbons replied. And he did!

After years of appeals the case came before the Justices. The question was, Did Mr. Gibbons' license from the Federal Government allow him to sail in New York waters in spite of the monopoly?

The Supreme Court found the answer in the commerce clause of the Constitution. "Congress shall have power to regulate commerce with foreign nations, and among the several states."

"Commerce," said Chief Justice Marshall, "implies transportation. Therefore, the Federal Government, not the state, has the right to make laws concerning transportation on the nation's rivers. Mr. Gibbons has a federal license to transport goods. New York State cannot prevent him from doing so."

When John Marshall reached his seventy-first birthday on September 24, 1826, he was strong and vigorous. Just as his brother James had predicted many years before, John still enjoyed a good game of quoits.

But many of the men John Marshall had known were

now dead. Earlier, on July 4, both Thomas Jefferson and John Adams had died within hours of each other.

There had been many changes in government. Two new political parties had arisen. One took the name of the National Republicans, led by Henry Clay, of Kentucky. The other, a liberal party, along the lines of Jeffersonian policies, was called Democratic-Republican. This party was led by Andrew Jackson, of Tennessee.

"Jackson is too liberal for me. I'm afraid his liberal ideas will weaken the Government," said Marshall.

For the first time since 1804 and the Jefferson election, Chief Justice John Marshall let his political opinions be known. It did little to sway the voters. The popular General Jackson was elected.

John Marshall was immediately discouraged by the lawless way the Americans and the new President dealt with the Indians.

"There's plenty of land out west. Let the Indians go there," was President Jackson's opinion. "These tribes refuse to abide by the laws of the states in which we allow them to live. This causes confusion. The Indians should get out."

Again and again Jackson had helped push Indian nations beyond the Western frontiers.

"What President Jackson doesn't realize is that these Indian people are being forced to leave their homes and the land they love. It is a terrible tragedy to them to have to settle again in a strange place. Many would rather die," said John.

In President Jackson's opinion this was not such a

bad idea. As far as he was concerned, the fewer Indians the better.

Marshall found that he could not devote all his time to the conflict between the American Indians and the Government. John Marshall was ill. After many months of suffering, he traveled to Philadelphia, where he underwent a difficult operation. Fortunately, he soon recovered. But when he went home in December of 1831, he found that Polly was desperately sick.

On Christmas Day she took the locket she always wore and gave it to John. With tears in his eyes John fastened the delicate gold chain around his own neck.

"Wear it for me, John," whispered Polly. "That way I will always be near you."

A few hours later, Polly died.

John never fully recovered from the deep sadness he felt at losing Polly. They had been happily married for nearly forty-nine years.

Work, he felt, was the best medicine for him. John Marshall returned to Washington. There the Indian problem was causing quite a stir. Cherokee representatives came to the capital wearing fringed jackets and moccasins. People were frightened.

"It's an uprising!" some said. "The Indians are banding together."

"A handful of Cherokee is hardly a war party," John protested whenever he heard these foolish rumors. But horrible stories of Indian wars were being told everywhere in Washington.

Actually the Cherokee had come to appeal to the Supreme Court. When John Quincy Adams was

President, he had encouraged a man named Samuel Worcester to work with the Cherokee. Mr. Worcester had developed schools and work programs among the Indians. Now the State of Georgia in which the Cherokee lived objected. "Why, the Indians don't even obey state laws. With the help of men like Worcester they may rise up and murder us in our beds."

Mr. Worcester was forbidden to continue his work. When he refused to stop, officials arrested him.

The Court came to a decision quickly: "Mr. Worcester had every right to continue his work among the people of the Cherokee nation. The Cherokee were protected by federal law. Georgia has no right to interfere. Mr. Worcester should be released at once and allowed to continue his work."

For the first time a Supreme Court decision was completely ignored.

"John Marshall has made his decision," President Jackson reportedly said. "Now let him enforce it."

Discouraged and lonely without Polly, John spent the summer with his son James's family on part of the Fairfax lands he had purchased so long ago. By now he had twenty-seven lively grandchildren. They brightened his days.

When Chief Justice John Marshall was seventy-nine years old, he still continued to travel about to hold circuit court. On one trip his stagecoach overturned. Marshall was badly injured. Three of his sons took him to Philadelphia to seek the best medical advice. It was no use. On July 6, 1835, John Marshall died.

Bells in churches all over Philadelphia tolled as thousands of friends poured into the city to attend memorial services for the beloved Chief Justice.

High up in Independence Hall the great bell had proclaimed our nation's liberty in 1776, and now it rang for the last time. Like the giant heart of the free people of the country John Marshall loved so dearly, it cracked and was heard no more.

In its place rose new sounds of freedom. These were the courageous court decisions made by the man whose vision of freedom and responsibility reached far beyond his time.

# *Bibliography*

Beveridge, Albert J., *The Life of John Marshall.* 4 vols. Houghton Mifflin Company, 1916–1919.

Dunne, Gerald T., *Justice Joseph Story and the Rise of the Supreme Court.* Simon and Schuster, 1971.

Kurland, Philip B. (ed.), *James Bradley Thayer, Oliver Wendell Holmes and Felix Frankfurter on John Marshall.* The University of Chicago Press, 1967.

Mason, Frances Norton, *My Dearest Polly: Letters of Chief Justice John Marshall to His Wife, with Their Background, Political and Domestic, 1779–1831.*Garrett & Massie, Inc., 1961.

Severn, Bill, *John Marshall: The Man Who Made the Court Supreme.* David McKay Company, Inc., 1969.

Surrency, Edwin C. (ed.), *The Marshall Reader: The Life and Contributions of Chief Justice John Marshall.* Oceana Publications, 1955.